I0201452

The Officers' Handbook

Revised

A Guide For Officers In Young People's Societies, With Chapters On Parliamentary Law And Other Useful Themes

By

Amos R. Wells

First Fruits Press
Wilmore, Kentucky
c2015

The officers' handbook: a guide for officers in young people's societies, with chapters on parliamentary law and other useful themes, by Amos R. Wells.

First Fruits Press, ©2015
Previously published: Boston and Chicago: United Society of Christian Endeavor, ©1911.

ISBN: 9781621713975 (print), 9781621713982 (digital)

Digital version at http://place.asburyseminary.edu/christianendeavorbooks/22/

First Fruits Press is a digital imprint of the Asbury Theological Seminary, B.L. Fisher Library. Asbury Theological Seminary is the legal owner of the material previously published by the Pentecostal Publishing Co. and reserves the right to release new editions of this material as well as new material produced by Asbury Theological Seminary. Its publications are available for noncommercial and educational uses, such as research, teaching and private study. First Fruits Press has licensed the digital version of this work under the Creative Commons Attribution Noncommercial 3.0 United States License. To view a copy of this license, visit http://creativecommons.org/licenses/by-nc/3.0/us/.

For all other uses, contact:

First Fruits Press
B.L. Fisher Library
Asbury Theological Seminary
204 N. Lexington Ave.
Wilmore, KY 40390
http://place.asburyseminary.edu/firstfruits

Wells, Amos R. (Amos Russel), 1862-1933.
    The officers' handbook: a guide for officers in young people's societies, with chapters on parliamentary law and other useful themes / by Amos R. Wells.
    143 pages ; 21 cm.
    Revised.
    Wilmore, Ky. : First Fruits Press, ©2015.
    Reprint. Previously published: Boston : United Society of Christian Endeavor, ©1911.
    ISBN: 9781621713975 (pbk.)
    1. International Society of Christian Endeavor. 2. Parliamentary practice. I. Title.
BV1426 .W485 2015

Cover design by Jonathan Ramsay

asburyseminary.edu
800.2ASBURY
204 North Lexington Avenue
Wilmore, Kentucky 40390

First Fruits
THE ACADEMIC OPEN PRESS OF ASBURY SEMINARY

First Fruits Press
The Academic Open Press of Asbury Theological Seminary
204 N. Lexington Ave., Wilmore, KY 40390
859-858-2236
first.fruits@asburyseminary.edu
asbury.to/firstfruits

THE

OFFICERS' HANDBOOK

REVISED

A GUIDE FOR OFFICERS IN YOUNG PEOPLE'S SOCIETIES, WITH CHAPTERS ON PARLIAMENTARY LAW AND OTHER USEFUL THEMES

By AMOS R. WELLS

BOSTON AND CHICAGO
UNITED SOCIETY OF CHRISTIAN ENDEAVOR

Copyright, 1900 and 1911

BY

THE UNITED SOCIETY OF CHRISTIAN ENDEAVOR

1

CONTENTS.

CONTENTS

THE OFFICERS' HANDBOOK.

CHAPTER I.

THE KING'S BUSINESS.

CHRISTIAN ENDEAVOR is a spiritual movement and its heart is the prayer meeting, and yet it is as impossible to have a good society without a good business meeting, as to have a good business meeting without a good society. The spiritual side of the work grows as the committee work grows, and the society's activity increases as the spiritual fervor increases, each depending on the other. Uplifting prayer meetings are the result of good work on the part of the prayer-meeting committee, and that committee in turn is stimulated to better work by uplifting prayer meetings. Souls are won to Christ by the zealous labors of the lookout committee, and evangelistic zeal, once implanted in a society, will spur the lookout committee to unselfish endeavors. If the consecration meetings are genuine, the business meetings will be enthusiastic and practical.

But if neither of these things is true? At which

5

end shall we begin to work? Shall we first make the body, and then pour into it the breath of life? Or shall we seek first the motive and later supply the machinery?

There is no need of deciding, for we are to work toward both ends at the same time. This book illustrates, therefore, only one side of a successful society, and what some might call the lower side, if there were any higher or lower in religious work. For the other side, I must refer the Endeavorer to the volume in this series that deals with "Prayer-Meeting Methods," and to the numbers of the "Ways of Working Series" entitled "On the Lookout" and "Our Crowning Meeting." Throughout this book I must take it for granted that the reader understands that the society mechanism is only a means toward an end, and that all Endeavorers know what is the great object for which alone Christian Endeavor business is conducted, and what is the pervading spirit in which alone it will succeed.

Therefore I do not at all sympathize with those that would minimize the business in our society work. Do not be petty and fussy. Do not spend time in polishing the locomotive when you should be on the road. Do not exalt the way above the goal, the method above the object. But, on the other hand, magnify your office, enlarge it with the thoroughness of a Paul. Complete the business to the finger nails, as carefully as Angelo would finish a statue. Be ashamed of a short business meeting. **If you** have little business, it means little committee work. And be ashamed of a dull business meeting. It means that your society is half asleep.

And our Christian Endeavor business should be done in the very best way. We are "about our Father's business." How punctilious are all that do business for a king! Letters presented to him must be handsomely engrossed. The most minute act regarding his wardrobe, his food, his bed, must be performed with perfect care and according to the strictest rule. How attentive to details are lovers that execute commissions for their sweethearts! No least slip is permitted in accuracy, in fineness, in promptness, in grace. If we truly love God, and serve Him as our King, we shall count nothing too good for His service. His wish will be enough for us, as David's wish for the water by Bethlehem's gate was enough for his strong men. Whatever is worth doing is worth doing well, and whatever God wants done is worth doing. If in his public prayers, and even when he prays in secret, a Christian will take pains to use only the choicest words, why should he not also be careful to use only the most fitting and up-to-date methods in all his religious labors? Let us be workmen that need not to be ashamed. Let us permit no slovenly work about the King's business—not even in the King's kitchen.

Verily, we want God to toil for us; and oh, how He labors! Look at the business meeting of the spring. What motions are passed by the breezes! How eagerly the fields resolve themselves into committees of the whole! What a music committee are the birds, what a flower committee is active

through the woods! What a vigilant lookout committee has its headquarters among the clouds.
What a summer business meeting! And what a
fall business meeting! Yes, and what a winter
business meeting, too, though all its work is done
so quietly. And in the presence of this abounding
energy of God, that spends itself upon us so lavishly
and continually, shall we find it onerous to attend
one committee meeting a fortnight?

Ah, let us be "diligent in business"! That shall
be the motto of this book. That can be our spirit,
only as we *enjoy* our Christian activities. "Diligent"
comes from the Latin words meaning to chooso
out, to love; and however we may lash ourselves
with the whip of conscience and the thong of duty,
we are not truly diligent, but only pretending to
be, until we have come—possibly by dint at first of
mere duty-doing—to love our work.

The King's business requireth haste. Why? Because the night cometh, when no man can work.
The knowledge of the extreme brevity even of the
longest life, the thought of the vast reaches of eternity, the consciousness that upon our life here depend the eternal issues for us and for others—no
one can entertain these great ideas without being
spurred thereby to an activity so fierce that it would
speedily burn his life out were it not for the peace
and quietness our Master gives His followers. That
peace enters our souls and takes away all fretfulness
and fever from our toil, while, none the less, we
seek the Kingdom first of all, and it is our meat
and our drink to do the will of the Father.

CHAPTER II.

CHRISTIAN ENDEAVOR FUNDAMENTALS.

THE officers of our Christian Endeavor societies are the local leaders of the Christian Endeavor movement. The State and national leaders cannot go far with their voices, and only a little farther with their pens; but the local leaders, in the aggregate, go everywhere. It is of supreme importance, therefore, if the movement is to flourish, that all our Christian Endeavor officers shall be able to defend it against criticism, and to show why they believe in it, what good it is doing, and what are its purposes and principal methods. A chapter on Christian Endeavor fundamentals, then, stands appropriately at the opening of this officers' handbook.

What are the Christian Endeavor essentials? What constitutes an Endeavor society? How is it differentiated from the old type of young people's meetings that made so manifest a failure?

From the beginning, in 1881, six features have characterized the Society. In spite of hundreds of improved methods that since have been added, in spite of the adoption of many new interests and the completing of many noble achievements, these six characteristics are still the summary of the Society. They have proved their value by the test of time and experience.   Societies that lacked them have quietly passed away ; societies that possessed them have grown and are yet growing.   Formally emphasized in many written and spoken addresses, they have come to be recognized everywhere as Christian Endeavor principles, and no Christian Endeavor officer should be ignorant either of what they are, or of their profound and fundamental meaning.

First of these principles stands the pledge.   Primarily not the particular form of words set forth by the United Society ; no stress has ever been laid upon that ; the United Society has itself revised them, and different countries have varied from them. The pledge idea, however, is essential to a society of Christian Endeavor—the willingness, upon recognizing that Christ wants us to do certain things, to promise to do them, and to enter into open covenant for that purpose.   This idea all our Christian Endeavor officers should be prepared to defend and advocate.   If any one objects that this takes away from the freedom of a Christian, they should be quick to reply that Christian freedom consists in doing the will of Christ, and that the only question to be settled is whether the pledge unfolds a part of Christ's will or not.   If any one objects that it is impossible to keep the pledge, they should be prompt to direct attention to the provision for excuses ; nothing is promised without the proviso, " unless prevented by some reason which I can conscientiously give to my Saviour."   The pledge simply agrees to testify for Christ, attend to the society's committee work, pray and read the Bible daily, and support the church and its services—*unless* we have some excuse we think Christ would accept. When our officers ask the critics, "Does not Christ want us to do these things?" they must answer, "Yes, as a general thing." "Then why not promise Him that we *will* do them, when He wants us to do them?" The pledge makes firm, conscientious Christians. It educates young people in promise-keeping—a training much needed in our modern times. It has been the backbone of the Christian Endeavor movement, and any society that grows lax in regard to it, will grow lax in everything else.

Our second fundamental is the monthly roll-call meeting, first named the experience meeting, now usually named the consecration meeting. Why is it an essential? Because it serves as a test of fidelity to the pledge, a constant reminder of it, a spur to fulfilling it. To send a message, if one must be absent, and to testify in answer to one's name, if present—this, once a month, is obviously no unreasonable burden, and if one is unwilling to do this much, not even he himself would think that he ought to be kept in the society. Through the consecration meeting, therefore, the profitless members are weeded out, and the society is kept to its standard of efficiency. Our Christian Endeavor officers, having this understanding of the purpose of the meeting, will be ready to answer the criticism often leveled against the society because of a misunderstanding of our use of the term, "consecration," and because of the testimony sometimes heard at this meeting, "I want to re-consecrate myself." Christian Endeavorers understand that consecration to God, made once, is made forever; that it is not an act to be repeated month after month; and by our "consecration meeting" we mean only a meeting to bring out new elements in the consecration we have already made, to remind ourselves of it, to report our experiences concerning it, to emphasize the pledge of consecration we have taken upon ourselves. A meeting for this purpose once a month is none too often, and has infused into our society an element of strength to be obtained in no other way.

In the third place, Christian Endeavor believes in systematic, definite, regular committee work. Why? Because the main purpose of the society is to train young Christians for the church, and there is no way to learn how to do things without doing them. The advantages of our Christian Endeavor committee work, so varied, so extensive, so practical, so helpful, are sufficiently manifest, and our officers will not need to dilate upon them. They need only to remember that all of it is an outgrowth of Christian Endeavor, developed as the Society developed, and unknown before to the young people of the world.

Private devotion is the fourth plank of our society platform—daily prayer and daily Bible-reading. Like all the rest of the pledge, this part is flexible. It is left for the individual conscience, kept in touch with its Lord, to dictate how long and when one is to pray, and how much of the Bible shall be read daily, and in what way it shall be studied. Here, too, as throughout the pledge, the provision regarding reasonable excuses is in force. Nevertheless, Christian Endeavor believes that it is impossible to maintain in power the outer exercises of religion unless we maintain with fervor this private communion with God, and by courses of Bible-study, and by the Quiet Hour pledge of at least fifteen minutes in the early morning for meditation and prayer, and in many other ways, the Society is constantly reminding its members that their only strength for any work comes from on high, and must be drawn from the reservoirs of prayer.

Denominational loyalty is the fifth Christian Endeavor principle—a principle to which all experience shows that the young people are true. The pledge indicates general church-support, and, in particular, attendance on the midweek prayer meeting and the Sunday evening service as ways in which this denominational loyalty may be exhibited. It has been shown frequently that the Endeavorers are faithful to their promises in these points. In larger numbers, proportionately, than the older church members, they are to be found at the Sunday evening service and the midweek prayer meeting. They are loyal to their denominational missions and church periodicals. Where their denomination has formed a separatist young people's society, they have even carried this principle so far as to commit suicide as an Endeavor society, and drop sadly out of the Christian Endeavor fellowship. The "forward movements" in Christian Endeavor, like the Tenth Legion and the Macedonian Phalanx, have all been for the sole benefit of the denominations. Many thousands of pastors are constantly testifying to the Endeavorers' loyalty.

Sixth and last in the list of Christian Endeavor principles is interdenominational fellowship. Christian Endeavor has developed a very complete and beautiful system of unions—city, county, State, national, and world-wide. In most communities these unions are the only rallying centers for the Christians of all faiths. Everywhere they are powerful agencies for co-operative action, and delightful promoters of a mutual understanding and brotherly helpfulness. Endeavorers know that from this source they gain vast enthusiasm, that their union work serves to popularize good methods, and that, best of all, in this coming together they are hastening the fulfilment of Christ's command and prayer, "that they all may be one." Our officers should understand the dangers that attend this union work, watching jealously that nothing is admitted prejudicial to denominational loyalty. They will see that their union is furnished with a Pastors' Advisory Committee, and in all their relations with other societies they will be guided by their pastors' wise control. Yet they will not forget how great and blessed is Christian Endeavor's responsibility for the perpetuation and enlarging of this fellowship. They will see the coming glories of the federation of the churches. They will believe in church union— just as close a union as is possible without violating consciences. And for this ideal they will be glad to work.

These, then, are the six objects of Christian

Endeavor. From these essentials all other purposes of the Society spring, and to them they are subordinate. Compare the church, as Christ compared it, to a vineyard. Then the pledge is the stake to which the tender, pliant vine is tied. The consecration meeting is the rain poured upon it from above. Private devotions are the foodful soil, strong with its beautiful hidden strength. The committee work is the tilling of the plant. Denominational loyalty is the trellis along which the vines run from stake to stake. Interdenominational fellowship is the entire vineyard, the wind and the rain and the snow that fall upon the whole, the wise plans for the vineyard, for plowing and fertilizing, for keeping off insects, for pruning, for gathering the fruit. How foolish to shut each vine up in a separate coop!

The church has scarcely begun to realize what blessings will come to her from this access of ardent, well-trained young workers. The pledge has given them spiritual stamina, the consecration meeting has given them the virtue of continuance. Private devotions have given them depth. Committee work has made them practical. Labor for their denomitions has made them intense. Fellowship with other denominations has made them broad. As our Christian Endeavor officers come to understand better and better the purposes of our noble organization, the results it has already achieved and the still grander results it is sure to achieve in the opening future, they will believe in the Society with all their hearts, and they will work for it with all their might.

CHAPTER III.

THE CONSTITUTION AND BY-LAWS.

WHAT is known as the "Model Constitution" for Christian Endeavor societies—that furnished by the United Society of Christian Endeavor and used in organizing new societies, though substantially the same as that formed for Dr. Clark's pioneer society in Williston Church, Portland, Maine, has received several revisions, and is now sent out in the following form. Always when it is sent out, however, there goes with it the statement that it is put forth only as a recommendation, and that, though it is hoped that its main principles may everywhere be adopted, the societies are perfectly free to make whatever changes are needed to adapt it to local needs. The constitution itself deals with general principles, and it is best for the society to take it without modification, while the by-laws represent the more variable factors, and it is they that may more wisely be changed. It is not to be forgotten, however, what constitutes a Christian Endeavor society, and no modification should be made that will annul any of the six principles stated in the preceding chapter—principles that have confirmed themselves now by the experience of so many years and of so many thousand societies all over the world.

In this chapter I shall present the Model Constitu•

tion, in company with such explanatory notes as my experience in answering innumerable questions, both at conventions and in the columns of *The Christian Endeavor World*, has shown to be helpful and needed.

THE MODEL CONSTITUTION.

ARTICLE I. — *Name.*

This society shall be called the................
YOUNG PEOPLE'S SOCIETY OF CHRISTIAN ENDEAVOR.

[Some societies have a double name. The society to which Dr. Clark now belongs, for instance, is called "The Golden Rule Society of Christian Endeavor," or, "The Congregational Society of Christian Endeavor, of Auburndale, Mass."]

ARTICLE II. — *Object.*

Its object shall be to promote an earnest Christian life among its members, to increase their mutual acquaintance, to train them for work in the church, and in every way to make them more useful in the service of God.

[Four objects, it will be observed. Have you paid much attention to this section? Why not print it in large letters and hang it before the society with the purpose henceforth of developing the members along all three lines?]

ARTICLE III. — *Membership.*

1. The members shall consist of four classes: Active, Associate, Affiliated, and Honorary.

2. *Active Members.* The active members of this society shall consist of young persons who believe themselves to be Christians, and who sincerely desire to accomplish the objects above specified. It is left for each society and Pastor to determine whether or not active members must be members of the church.

[Of course the word, "young," may have some exceptions, and may include those that are young in the Christian life and need the training of the society. It is here used, however, to shut out mature and experienced Christians who should be working in the other portions of the church, and for whom, if they wish to show an interest in the young people's society, a place is made as honorary members.

It is often asked whether the active membership of the society should be confined to church-members. I myself came to be a church-member through service as an active Endeavorer, and I know of many more that were thus brought into the church, so that my personal belief on this point may easily be guessed. On the other hand, there are many wise and experienced pastors who think that since all "who believe themselves to be Christians" *should* join the church, it would be a great mistake to allow them to become active Endeavorers without first taking that step. On this point, therefore, since the opinions of pastors and the practice of the societies are so divided, no recommendation is made in the Model Constitution, but the pastor and church are left to adopt the course that seems best.]

3. *Associate Members.* All young persons of worthy character, who are not at present willing to be considered decided Christians, may become associate members of this society. It is expected that all associate members will habitually attend the prayer meetings, and that they will in time become active members, and the society will work to this end.

[It will be noticed that the associate members are by this definition those that are not willing to be considered Christians. No church-member, therefore, should under any circumstances be permitted to join as an associate member. The associate members should not lead the meetings, nor serve as chairmen of the committees, nor, indeed, should they be placed upon any of the committees that have charge of the distinctively spiritual interests of the society, such as the prayer-meeting and lookout committees. If their names are called at the consecration meetings, they should not be expected to make any response except "Present," though of course all would be glad to have them testify at that time; and their names should be called in a list by themselves, before the roll of active members.]

4. *Affiliated Members.* In order to reach and establish a point of contact with young people who for any reason will not join the society, clubs or classes of any kind, such as civic, athletic, musical, literary, Bible-study, and mission-study, may be organized under the leadership of the Endeavorers, and the members of these clubs shall be accepted as affiliated members of the society. It is hoped

that they may soon become active members, and
the society will labor to that end.

5. *Honorary Members.* All persons who, though
no longer young, are still interested in the society,
and wish to have some connection with it, though
they cannot regularly attend the meetings, may
become honorary members. Their names shall
be kept upon the list under the appropriate heading,
but shall not be called at the roll-call meeting. It
is understood that the society may look to them
for financial and moral support in all worthy efforts.
(For a special class of honorary members, see Article
X.)

[This class of members is made up of older Christians that enjoy the Christian Endeavor meetings,
and wish to be in close touch with the society for
the sake of helping it along. The class is also for
those that have served for a term of years in the
society and, graduating from it to take up the full
duty of the older portion of the church, desire to
retain some connection with the work they have
come to love. No young person' whose circumstances do not forbid his becoming an active or
an associate member should be allowed to become
an honorary member.]

6. These different persons shall become members,
upon being elected by the society, after carefully
examining the Constitution and upon signing their
names to it, thereby pledging themselves to live up
to its requirements. Voting power shall be vested
in the active members and in the members of the
affiliated groups who may be professing Christians.

ARTICLE IV. — *Officers.*

1. The officers of this society shall be a President, Vice-President, Recording Secretary, Corresponding Secretary, and Treasurer, who shall be chosen from among the active members of the society.

[Of course, other officers may be added. Some societies will wish to include the organist in this list. Some societies of small membership give the offices of recording secretary and treasurer to the same person.]

2. There shall also be a Lookout Committee, a Prayer-Meeting Committee, a Social Committee, and such other committees as the needs of each society may require, each consisting of five active members, unless otherwise determined. There shall also be an Executive Committee, as provided in Article VI.

[The number of members to be placed upon a committee must vary with the size of the society, three being the minimum for an efficient committee. Some societies have the excellent custom of placing each member on a committee, assigning each new member also to a committee as soon as he is elected.]

ARTICLE V. — *Duties of Officers.*

1. *President.* The President of the society shall perform the duties usually pertaining to that office. He shall have especial watch over the interests of the society, and it shall be his care to see that the different committees perform the duties devolving

upon them. He shall be chairman of the Executive Committee.

2. *Vice-President.* In the absence of the President, the Vice-President shall perform his duties.

[A foot-note to the Model Constitution suggests that the vice-president may also be chairman of the lookout committee — a wise suggestion.]

3. *Corresponding Secretary.* It shall be the duty of the Corresponding Secretary to keep the local society in communication with the United Society, and with the local and State unions, and to present to his own society such matters of interest as may come from the United Society, and other authorized sources of Christian Endeavor information. This office should be retained by one person as long as its duties can be efficiently performed, and the name shall be forwarded to the United Society.

[The somewhat common complaint in regard to the efficiency of this officer is doubtless warranted, but the cause lies back of the corresponding secretaries, in the members of the societies themselves, who do not realize the importance of the post, nor understand what qualifications are required, and therefore do not see to it that the position is appropriately filled. See the chapter on the corresponding secretary.]

4. *Recording Secretary.* It shall be the duty of the Recording Secretary to keep a roll of the members, to correct it from time to time, as may be necessary, and to obtain the signature to the Constitution of each newly elected member; also to correspond with absent members, and to inform

them of their standing in the society; also to keep correct minutes of all business meetings of the society and of the Executive Committee; also to notify all persons elected to office or to committees, and to do so in writing, if necessary.

[It might be thought that the corresponding with absent members should belong to the corresponding secretary, and so it should, on any other subject; but the recording secretary has the records, and is the more suitable person to spur the absent members to their duty, unless, indeed, the lookout committee undertake this delicate task. It should be noted that the secretary may not correct the list of members on his own authority, but only after the vote of the lookout committee.]

5. *Treasurer.* It shall be the duty of the Treasurer to keep safely all money belonging to the society, and to pay out only such sums as shall be voted by the society, or the committees as authorized by the society.

[Of course the society or the executive committee may give permission to certain committees to draw on the treasurer for the needs of their work, and it is not customary for the society to vote upon slight and habitual payments, as for topic cards, postage, and little expenses attending the socials, but only on the disposition of large sums, such as the gifts to missions, or of small sums when they are to go in unusual ways. Strictly, too, the treasurer should pay out money only on written order from the secretary, but in practice this formality is generally dispensed with.]

ARTICLE VI. — *Duties of Committees.*

1. *Lookout Committee.* It shall be the duty of this committee to bring new members into the society, to introduce them to the work and to the other members, and affectionately to look after and reclaim any that seem indifferent to their duties, as outlined in the pledge. This committee shall also, by personal investigation, satisfy itself of the fitness of young persons to become members of this society, and shall propose their names at least one week before the society votes upon their election.

[It is especially necessary that the new members understand what they promise in the pledge. The lookout committee should have each of them read the pledge, and should question him upon it, clause by clause, making sure that he comprehends each section, and means to abide by it.]

2. *Prayer-Meeting Committee.* It shall be the duty of this committee to have in charge the prayer meeting, to see that a topic is assigned and a leader appointed for every meeting, and to do what it can to make the meetings interesting and helpful.

3. *Missionary Committee.* It shall be the duty of this committee to provide for regular missionary meetings, to organize mission-study classes when feasible, to interest the members of the society in missionary topics, and to aid, in any manner which may seem practicable, the cause of home and foreign missions.

4. *Social Committee.* It shall be the duty of this committee to promote the social interests of the

society by welcoming strangers to the meetings, and by providing for the mutual acquaintance of the members by occasional socials, for which any appropriate entertainment, of which the church approves, may be provided.

[There can never be just criticism of our socials if the clause, "of which the church approves," is followed out. All plans for socials should be submitted, in outline, at least, to the pastor.]

5. *Executive Committee.* This committee shall consist of the Pastor of the church, the officers of the society, the chairmen of the various committees, and the leaders of affiliated groups or clubs. All matters of business requiring debate shall be brought first before this committee, and by it reported to the society. All discussion of proposed measures should take place before this committee, and not before the society. Recommendations concerning the finances of the society should also originate with this committee.

[It has been observed in Article V. that the president is chairman of this committee. The committee should meet regularly, at least once a month, before the monthly business meeting. The object of the committee is two-fold: "To prevent waste of time in the regular meeting of the society by useless debate and unnecessary parliamentary practice, which are always harmful to the spirit of the prayer meeting," and also to counsel together concerning the society work. See the chapter on this important committee.]

6. Each committee, except the Executive, shall

make a report in writing to the society, at the monthly business meetings, concerning the work of the past month.

[The recording secretary generally keeps these reports on file. The executive committee also may properly present a report, as outlined elsewhere.]

ARTICLE VII. — *The Prayer Meeting.*

All the active members shall attend and heartily support every meeting, unless prevented by some reason which can conscientiously be given to their Master, Jesus Christ.

[Of course the common sense of the society must be exercised to determine what is "hearty support" of the meeting. The pledge itself shuts out singing as a sufficient participation. The mere calling for a hymn to be sung, without adding any word of personal testimony, or the mere answering of "Present" at the roll-call, should not be considered as meeting this requirement.]

ARTICLE VIII. — *The Pledge.*

All persons on becoming active members of the Society shall sign the Active Member's Pledge. Associate members shall sign the Associate Member's Pledge.

[The Model Constitution gives in an appendix the following samples of various forms of pledge in use, from which a selection can be made:

FORM I. — ACTIVE MEMBER'S PLEDGE.

Trusting in the Lord Jesus Christ for strength, I promise Him that I will strive to do whatever He would like to have me do; that I will pray to Him and read the Bible every day; and that, just so far as I know how, throughout my whole life, I will endeavor to lead a Christian life. As an Active Member, I promise to be true to all my duties, to be present at, and take some part, aside from singing, in every meeting, unless hindered by some reason which I can conscientiously give to my Lord and Master, Jesus Christ. If obliged to be absent from the monthly consecration meeting, I will, if possible, send an excuse for absence to the Society.

Signed......................

FORM 2. — ACTIVE MEMBER'S PLEDGE.

Trusting in the Lord Jesus Christ for strength, I promise Him that I will strive to do whatever He would like to have me do; that I will make it the rule of my life to pray and read the Bible every day, and to support my own church in every way, especially by attending all her regular Sunday and mid-week services, unless prevented by some reason which I can conscientiously give to my Saviour; and that, just so far as I know how, throughout my whole life, I will endeavor to lead a Christian life.

As an Active Member, I promise to be true to all my duties, to be present at and to take some part, aside from singing, in every Christian Endeavor prayer meeting, unless hindered by some reason which I can conscientiously give to my Lord and Master. If obliged to be absent from the monthly consecration meeting of the Society, I will, if possible, send at least a verse of Scripture to be read in response to my name at the roll-call.

Signed......................

FORM 3. — ACTIVE MEMBER'S PLEDGE.

Trusting in the Lord Jesus Christ for strength, I promise Him that I will strive to do whatever He would have me do. I will make it the rule of my life to pray and read the Bible, to support the work and worship of my church, and to take my part in the meetings and other activities of this society. I will seek to bring others to Christ, to give as I can for the spread of the Kingdom, to advance my country's welfare, and promote the Christian brotherhood of man. These things I will do unless hindered by conscientious reasons, and in them all I will seek the Saviour's guidance.

Signed......................

FORM 4. — ACTIVE MEMBER'S PLEDGE.

Trusting in the Lord Jesus Christ for strength, I promise Him that I will strive to do whatever He would have me do. I will make it the rule of my life to pray and read the Bible, to support the work and worship of my church, and to take my part in the meetings and other activities of this society. These things I will do unless hindered by conscientious reasons, and in them all I will seek the Saviour's guidance.

Signed......................

FORM 5. — ASSOCIATE MEMBER'S PLEDGE.

As an Associate Member I promise to attend the prayer meetings of the Society habitually, and declare my willingness to do what I may be called upon to do as an Associate member to advance the interests of the Society.

Signed......................

The United Society adds here the foot-note:

"If none of these meets the local needs, the pastor and society are at liberty to formulate a pledge of their own; but it is earnestly hoped that a pledge embracing the ideas of private devotion, loyalty to the church, and outspoken confession of Christ in the weekly meeting will be adopted."]

ARTICLE IX. — *The Consecration Meeting.*

1. *Once each month, or as often as the society may decide, a consecration or covenant meeting may be held, at which the roll may be called, and the responses of the active members · shall be considered as renewed expressions of allegiance to Christ. It is expected that if any one is obliged to be · absent from this meeting, he will send a message, or at least a verse of Scripture, to be read in response to his name at the roll-call.*

[In regard to this, we should be careful to apply the section of our pledge in which we promise to try to do "whatever Christ would like to have us do." Certainly He wants us to make our prayer-meeting participation as helpful as possible, both to others and to ourselves, and generally the mere reading of a verse of Scripture without the addition of some word, however brief, to indicate that the passage is used to express the Endeavorer's feelings and experience, would not be the best possible mode of taking part in the meeting.

In a foot-note the Model Constitution recommends that the *first* meeting of each month be observed as consecration meeting.]

2. If any active member of this society is absent from this meeting, and fails to send a message, the Lookout Committee is expected to take the name of such a one, and in a kind and brotherly spirit ascertain the reason for the absence. *If any active member of the society is absent from three consecutive consecration meetings, without sending a*

message, the Lookout Committee and the Pastor shall consider the matter, and may recommend to the Executive Committee that the member be dropped from the roll.

[Note that the lookout committee is expected to investigate the very first unexplained absence, not to wait till there have been three of them. Note also that if the pastor, lookout committee, and executive committee decide to drop the member, no announcement whatever should be made before the society. The name should be quietly dropped by the secretary, and that is all.]

3. Any associate member who, without good reason, is regularly absent from the prayer meetings, and shows no interest whatever in the work of the society, may, upon recommendation of the Lookout Committee and Pastor to the Executive Committee, be dropped from the roll of members.

[This has no reference to the consecration meeting, since the associate member has made no promise concerning it. Hold on to the associate member as long as you think he is getting good from the society, and not doing a preponderating amount of harm.]

ARTICLE X. — *Relation to the Church.*

This society, being a part of the church, owes allegiance only and altogether to the church with which it is connected. The Pastors, Elders, Deacons, Stewards, and Sunday-school Superintendent, if not active members, shall be, *ex officiis*, honorary members. Any difficult question shall be laid before them for advice, and their decision shall be final. It shall be understood that the nomination or election of officers or other action taken by the society shall be subject to revision or veto by the church; that in every way the society shall put itself under the control of the official board of the church, and shall make a report to the church monthly, quarterly, or annually, as the church may direct.

[It is often asked whether the pastor should join as an active member. That depends entirely upon his other duties, and upon his judgment as to what course will be best for the society and the church. If he wishes to be an active member, should he be voted in like any other person? He will doubtless wish, for the sake of the example, to come in just as the others do. The report to the church should be made by the president or the secretary, as the church and the society prefer.]

ARTICLE XI. — *Relation of the Intermediate and Junior Societies.*

1. The Young People's Society of Christian Endeavor and the Junior Society being united by ties of closest sympathy and common effort, monthly (or at least annual) reports should be read to the Christian Endeavor Society by the Junior Superintendent. When the boys and girls reach the age of fourteen they may be transferred to the older society. Special pains shall be taken to see that a share of the duties and responsibilities of the prayer

meetings and of the general work of the society shall be borne by the younger members.

[In my opinion, the most helpful connection between the two societies is made by means of a "Junior committee" from the older society, which assists the Junior superintendent. Sometimes let a Junior report for his society at the monthly business meeting. If your church has an Intermediate society, the transfer at the age of fourteen will be to it, and the Young People's society will stand in the same relation to the Intermediates as to the Juniors.]

2. If the number of children and the other conditions call for the establishment of an Intermediate Society, the Juniors may be graduated into that society at the age of fourteen, and graduated from the Intermediate into the Young People's Society at the age of seventeen. The Superintendent of the Intermediate Society should report to the Young People's Society at the same time with the Junior Superintendent.

ARTICLE XII. — *Fellowship.*

This society, while owing allegiance only to its own church and denomination, is united by ties of spiritual fellowship with other Christian Endeavor societies the world around. This fellowship is based upon a common love to Christ, the principles of a common covenant, and common methods of work, and is guaranteed by a common name, "Christian Endeavor," used either alone or in connection with some denominational name.

This fellowship is that of an interdenominational,

not an undenominational, organization. It is pro-
moted by local-union meetings, State and national
conventions, and in many other ways.

[The compound name, such as "Epworth League
of Christian Endeavor," "Baptist Union of Christian
Endeavor," is extensively used. With the excep-
tion of only one denomination, Christian Endeavor
societies are permitted by their churches to belong
at the same time to their denominational union and
to the Christian Endeavor interdenominational fellowship.]

ARTICLE XIII. — *Withdrawals.*

Any member who may wish to withdraw from
the society shall state the reasons to the Lookout
Committee and Pastor. On their recommendation
to the Executive Committee, the member's name
may be dropped from the roll.

[No announcement is made of this withdrawal;
the secretary is simply instructed to drop the name
from the roll. Such a person, if he wishes to returr
to the society, must be voted in as if he had never
been a member.]

ARTICLE XIV. — *Expansion.*

Any other committees may be added and duties
assumed by this society which in the future may
seem best.

ARTICLE XV. — *Transfer of Members.*

Since it would in the end defeat the very object
of our organization if the older active members, who

have been trained in the society for usefulness in the church, should remain content with fulfilling their pledge to the society only, therefore it is expected that the older members, when it shall become impossible for them to attend two weekly prayer meetings, shall be transferred to the honorary membership of the society, if previously faithful to their vows as active members. This transfer, however, shall be made with the understanding that the obligation to faithful service shall still be binding upon them in the regular church prayer meeting. It shall be left to the Lookout Committee, in conjunction with the Pastor, to recommend to the society this transfer of membership.

[This is quite different from dropping a name from the roll, and as it is a step in Christian Endeavor which should be emphasized, it is desirable to recognize such graduation by some public exercise, such as is outlined in a later chapter of this book.]

ARTICLE XVI. — *Amendment.*

This Constitution may be amended at any regular business meeting, by a two-thirds vote of the entire active membership of the society, provided that a written statement of the proposed amendment shall have been read to the society and deposited with the Secretary at the regular business meeting next preceding.

BY-LAWS.

[These by-laws are only specimen rules, given as suggestions, to be adopted in whole or in part as the needs of each society require.]

ARTICLE I.

This society shall hold a prayer meeting on the .... evening of each week. The first regular prayer meeting of the month shall be a consecration meeting, at which the roll shall be called.

ARTICLE II.

Method of Conducting the Consecration Meeting.

At this meeting the roll may be called by the leader during the meeting or at its close. After the opening exercises, the names of five or more may be called, and then a hymn may be sung or a prayer offered. The committees may be called by themselves, the letters of the alphabet merely may be called (all whose names begin with A responding first, etc.), or other variations of the roll-call may be introduced. Thus varied, with singing and prayer interspersed, the entire roll shall be called. During the meeting, or at its close, the list of associate members may be called, the associates answering "Present."

ARTICLE III.

This society may hold its regular business meeting in connection with the .... regular prayer meeting in the month, or in connection with a monthly social. Special business meetings may be held at the call of the President.

["This business meeting," says a foot-note of the Model Constitution, "will usually be simply for the hearing of reports from the committees, or for such matters as will not detract from the spiritual tone of the meeting." All matters requiring discussion, it will be remembered, are to be brought before the executive committee, and not before the society. Of course this remark does not apply so closely to the business meetings that are not held in connection with the prayer meetings.

Since our Christian Endeavor business meetings are all concerned solely with religious matters, and with hearing the reports of religious work, they are not inappropriate to the Lord's Day if the society meets on that day. A full Christian Endeavor business meeting ought to be carried through within twenty minutes. It is better, however, to meet on some evening when more time can be obtained without encroaching upon the time of the prayer meeting, and not a few societies hold their business meetings in connection with their socials. The executive committee may call a business meeting through the president, or, in his absence, through the officer next in rank. A business meeting should be held every month, as indicated in Article VI., 6 of the Constitution, and a good plan is always to hold the business meeting on the last, and the consecration meeting on the first, Sunday of each month.]

ARTICLE IV.

The election of officers and committees shall be held at the first business meeting in..............

A Nominating Committee shall be appointed by the President at least two weeks previous to the time for electing new officers. Of this committee the Pastor shall be a member *ex officio*. If the society so orders, the officers and committee chairmen only may be elected, the new Executive Committee filling out the committees. It is understood that these officers are chosen subject to the approval of the church. If there is no objection on the part of the church, the election stands.

[Whether the election is held once a year or once in six months depends a little upon whether the society possesses an abundance of material sufficient to warrant semi-annual elections. The advantage of the nominating committee is that it insures a wise and careful review of the whole field, and previous conversations with the nominees to make sure that they will not refuse to serve. Nomination by this committee should be equivalent to an election, since it is not best or customary for the committee to present more than one name for each office. A struggle for votes among the friends of two candidates, however exciting and interesting, is not profitable in any way. It will be seen that the nominating committee is the most important committee of the year, and should be made up with great care. The pastor's presence upon it is very essential.]

ARTICLE V.

Applications for membership may be made on printed forms, which shall be supplied by the Lookout Committee and returned to them for consideration.

Names may be proposed for membership one week before the business meeting, and shall be voted on by the society at that meeting.

[Some societies think it more suitable and impressive to receive new members at the consecration meeting than at the business meeting. The best order, in my opinion, is for the names to be proposed at the business meeting, and voted upon at the consecration meeting which follows the next week, the new members being at once received into the society, and joining with the other members in repeating the pledge.]

ARTICLE VI.

Persons who have forfeited their membership may be re-admitted on recommendation of the Lookout Committee and Pastor, and by vote of the members present at any regular business meeting.

ARTICLE VII.

New members shall sign the Constitution within four weeks from their election, to confirm the vote of the society.

ARTICLE VIII.

Letters of introduction to other Christian Endeavor societies shall be given to members *in good standing* who apply to be released from their obligations to the society, this release to take effect when they shall become members of another society; until then, their names shall be kept on the Absent List. Members removing to other places, or desiring to join other Christian Endeavor societies in the same city or town, are requested to obtain letters of introduction within six months from the time of their leaving, unless they shall give satisfactory reasons to the society for their further delay.

[These letters of introduction do not take the place of regular election to membership, which must be done by the new society just as by the old.]

ARTICLE IX.

Other committees may be added, according to the needs of the society, of which the following are examples:

Information Committee. It shall be the duty of this committee to gather interesting and helpful information concerning Endeavorers or Endeavor work in all parts of the world, and to report the same. For this purpose, five minutes shall be set aside at the beginning of each meeting.

Sunday-School Committee. It shall be the duty of this committee to endeavor to bring into the Sunday school those who do not attend elsewhere, and to co-operate with the Superintendent and officers of the school in all ways which they may suggest for the benefit of the Sunday school.

Calling Committee. It shall be the duty of this committee to have a special care for those among the young people who do not feel at home in the church, to call on them, and to remind others where calls should be made.

Music Committee. It shall be the duty of this committee to provide for the singing at the young people's meeting, and also to turn the musical ability of the society to account when the Endeavorers can be helpful at public religious meetings.

Junior Committee. It shall be the duty of this committee to co-operate with the Superintendent of the Junior Society in every way, and in the absence of the Superintendent to see that a leader is secured and that the meetings are kept up.

Flower Committee. It shall be the duty of this committee to provide flowers for the pulpit, and to distribute them to the sick at the close of the Sabbath services.

Temperance Committee. It shall be the duty of this committee to do what may be deemed best to promote temperance principles and sentiment among the members of the society.

Relief Committee. It shall be the duty of this committee to do what it can to cheer and aid, by material comforts, if possible and necessary, the sick and destitute among the young people of the church and Sunday school.

Good-Literature Committee. It shall be the duty of this committee to do its utmost to promote the reading of good books and papers. To this end, it shall do what it can to circulate among its members the religious newspaper representing the society, also to obtain subscribers for the denominational papers and missionary magazines among the families of the congregation as the Pastor and church may direct. It may, if deemed best, distribute tracts and religious leaflets, and introduce good reading-matter in any other suitable way which may be desired.

Press Committee. It shall be the duty of this committee to send items regarding the work of the society and church to the newspapers accessible to it, and in all feasible ways to use for Christ the power of printers' ink.

The Whatsoever Committee. This committee shall consist of graduates from the Junior society, — all boys, if the society maintains also a Lend-a-Hand Committee. The Junior Superintendent shall be chairman of the committee, and its members shall aid the other committees in doing their work, take up the little duties that do not fall to the lot of any other committee, and in this way obtain an introduction to the work of the older society.

The Lend-a-Hand Committee. This committee, if it is formed, shall consist of the girl graduates from the Junior Society, and its work shall be similar to that of the Whatsoever Committee.

Other committees not here found may be added as occasion may demand and the church may desire.

[The Model Consitution adds in a foot-note:

Many societies find it a good plan to have so many committees that every member may serve on a committee or hold an office, thus receiving definite training by service."]

ARTICLE X.

Members who cannot meet with this society for a time are requested to obtain leave of absence, which shall be granted by the society and withdrawn at any time on recommendation of the Lookout Committee and Pastor, and their names shall be placed on the Absent List.

[Do not permit this "absent list" to become a catch-basket for the slothful. It is intended only for temporary absentees. If the member returns, notify him that he is restored to the regular list and is expected to return to his duties. If he is to be absent for a long time, suggest his joining a society where he is sojourning.]

ARTICLE XI.

.........members shall constitute a quorum.

[It is my opinion that a quorum should consist of a majority of the members, and if you cannot get a majority at your business meetings, you would better educate the society until you can.]

ARTICLE XII.

These By-Laws may be amended by a two-thirds vote of the members present at any regular meeting, provided that notice of such amendment is read to the society, and given in writing to the Secretary at least one week before the amendment is acted upon.

CHAPTER IV.

THE PRESIDENT'S WORK.

THERE is no characteristic of a good Christian worker that a Christian Endeavor president will not find useful in his important undertaking. If I were to name in order the qualities that are most essential, I should say consecration, judgment, tact, perseverance. Consecration, because his work will amount to nothing if it is done for himself or for the society; it must be done for God. Judgment, because it is as necessary for him to know what not to do as what to do, when to keep silent as when to speak, what plans to leave alone, as well as what to adopt; he needs a level head. Tact, because he is not to do things so much as to get them done, and all his plans will fail, and his consecration have slight result, if he does not know how to influence others and set them at work. Perseverance, because he will meet with many difficulties, because plans will not carry themselves out, and because one thing actually accomplished is better than many things merely begun or only desired.

In my opinion, the president should be a young man, not because a young man can always do the work better than a young woman, but because leadership is man's natural and God-appointed office, and because Christian Endeavor, like all good causes, has the young women any way, but must use every inducement to win and hold the boys and young men; and certainly they can be better won and held with a young man in the chair.

One of the president's most necessary qualifications is that he should not be afraid or reluctant to lead. Quietly and modestly he should keep the wheels in motion, propose plans, and see that they are carried out, and always take his rightful place in the forefront of society enterprises. All this, of course, should be done with the most entire openness to suggestions from others, and with constant remembrance of his fallibility. Lead them,—but do not be pig-headed and lead them into a pen.

The president must keep in intimate contact with all his officers and committeemen. He should work with the Junior superintendent as heartily as if he were—as he actually is—her assistant. Whether or not he is placed by the church upon its official board,—and, in my judgment, that recognition should be given him for more reasons than one,—the Christian Endeavor president should cultivate the closest relations with the pastor and the Sunday-school superintendent. He should know all the members of his society, and should prove himself a friend of all.

In every point the president should endeavor to make himself a model. He is a sort of pattern for the society, and his excellencies and defects will crop out in many unexpected places. He should add enthusiasm to the work of all the committees, pitching in and taking with them the first steps, at least, in all their enterprises. He should be ready to spend time and money in the society work. He should be the most social at the socials, and the most devout at the prayer meetings. He should by all means take part regularly in the church prayer meetings, and be a faithful Sunday-school worker. Let him prove by his own activities that Christian Endeavor does train a young Christian for all the work of the church. Though he should speak in every meeting, the president should not keep himself before the society with offensive prominence, but should make every appearance of his before the society tell, planning with care whatever he is to say, even to the announcement of a union meeting, and storing up for these utterances the best he can find of anecdote, quotation, the cream of his own thoughts and experiences.

Let me say in passing that it will be of the greatest helpfulness to the president if he carry with him a small note-book, especially and strictly reserved for memoranda of society plans and engagements.

Should the president accept re-election? That depends upon the condition of the society. If it is weak, with only a few possible leaders, it might be best for the president to serve for more than one term. Always, however, it must be the president's concern to train up some one to be his successor, and to retire just as soon as that successor is ready to step forward.

I have discussed in separate chapters the four most prominent phases of the president's activity,— namely, his work in the prayer meeting, his super-

intendence of the committees, his labors in connection with Christian Endeavor unions, and his conduct of the business meetings. To these chapters I
must ask those presidents to turn that honor me with
reading this book. In conclusion, however, let me
say that no labors in which you could possibly engage
would do more for you than this leadership in your
Christian Endeavor society. As you build up the
society, it will build you up. You will become a
more efficient speaker. You will gain ability in
business. You will develop tact, and priceless skill
in directing others. Courage and confidence will
come to you ; and with it all, and as the basis of it
all, you will be gaining power with God, which
underlies all genuine and noble power with men.
Is it not well worth while?

CHAPTER V.

THE PRESIDENT IN THE PRAYER MEETING.

THERE is a business meeting once a month, but there is a prayer meeting every week, and it is in the prayer meeting that the president can best impress the society with his ideas, and stimulate the members to better work. In the first place, if the society has the very helpful custom of holding with the leader a meeting for prayer before the regular meeting, he should be present with the prayer-meeting committee, and though the meeting should be led by the chairman of the prayer-meeting committee, he should inspire the little gathering all he can. Especially he should see that it does not hinder the following meeting, but is begun and closed on time.

It is well to establish in your society the custom of requiring the leaders always to call for items of business at the outset of the meeting, after the first song. If, however, you have not this custom, the president should always inform the leader beforehand when he has matters of business to present.

Since this preliminary business gives, in a sense, the keynote to the meeting, it is of importance that it should be well managed. It is an art to give out a notice in the best way. Do not read it. Have the points distinctly in mind. Do not introduce needless particulars, but give the essentials only, and nothing that does not concern the society. Repeat in different ways the chief points, such as the times and place of meetings, to which the society is invited. Be brisk, but not clownish. Be earnest, but never scold. Indeed, if you can get a little fun into these opening announcements, it will act like a tonic upon the meeting to follow.

In the meeting proper the president will constitute himself an unobtrusive, but none the less real, assistant leader. If the leader, for instance, fails to call on the information committee for its usual report, or forgets to save the pastor's five minutes at the end of the hour, the president will not hesitate to remind him of these matters. If a hymn is called for— whether by the leader, or by any one else—in an indistinct voice, he will ask for the announcement again, or, if he heard it, he will repeat it in a louder tone. If there is no music committee, he will not hesitate to start hymns impromptu. If a hymn is called for toward the close of the meeting, when time is precious, he will feel free to suggest that that hymn be held in reserve till the last. If the leader does not call for sentence prayers, the president will do so, beginning them himself. If he wants to encourage some of the faint-hearted members, he will cry, "Good!" after their testimonies; or, when some helpful thought has been uttered almost inaudibly by some frightened Endeavorer, he will repeat it, with a word of praise. Occasionally he will interject a pointed question to stimulate the discussion.

If there is any disorder, it is the president's duty to quell it at once. It is his duty, also, to see that the Endeavorers conduct themselves properly in the interval between their own meeting and the church meeting that follows. If there is no committee, such as the whatsoever committee, to whom this work might be assigned, the president will himself see that the room is ventilated, that the song-books are in the racks, and the chairs restored to order for the meeting. All points in which the society's good name is at stake should receive the president's jealous care.

If a stranger is present, the president should go to him at once, even during the meeting, and learn his name, tell him the evening's topic, and invite him to speak. To be sure, the social committee should do this, but the president, as representing the society, should not fail to do it also. Later in the meeting, if the person is one that will be ready to speak, the president should introduce him to the society and say how glad they will be for a few words from the stranger, either now or in the course of the meeting.

Equal attention should be paid, of course, to the older church members that may visit the society, and to the pastor. Indeed, it will do much to interest the church in the society if the president will make it a point to invite some one man or woman to attend each meeting and say a word to the young folks. The evening service of the church should always be announced in the Christian Endeavor society, and the president is the proper person to

4

make this announcement, coupling with it a hearty invitation to strangers, and emphasizing the pledge that all the members have taken.

As to his own testimony in the meeting, the president should study to make it a worthy model, for as a model it will certainly serve. Whether he prays or speaks, what he says should be earnest, brief, and right to the point. And let him not always take pains to stick to the topic, but let him often seize the opportunity to commend good committee work, or incorporate into his talk any especial advice or praise the society may need or deserve.

As early as possible in his term of office, the president should lead a prayer meeting, and on this occasion he will endeavor to sound the keynote of his administration, and push the society out along many lines of noble endeavor.

CHAPTER VI.

THE PRESIDENT AND THE COMMITTEES.

FOR purposes of oversight, suggestion, and inspiration, the president should consider himself a member of every committee in his society. He has a
right to attend every committee meeting, and he
should often and regularly exercise that right. This
will be difficult, unless he arranges for regularity in
committee meetings, not only as to time but as to
place, so that he may always know where to find a
certain committee meeting, and when. For instance, if his society has eight committees, he might
get them to meet once a month and two each week,
one on Tuesday and the other on Thursday, at 7 : 30
P. M., and always at the house of the chairman.
Once every month, then, or certainly once every
two months, the president might meet with each
committee.

Especially at the opening of the year's work, the
president should look after his committees with
care. It is a fine plan to invite them all to meet at
his house some evening. After some pleasant
opening exercises, including possibly a jolly little
address from the pastor, the committees will separate and consider in different rooms their work for
the coming term, the president and pastor going

about from group to group. After some time the
committees are called together, and each chairman
reports to the entire company the plans his committee has hit upon, these plans being followed by discussions. The same method may be applied to an
individual committee that is doing poor work : the
president may invite it to his house for an evening
of fresh suggestion and inspiration.

In all such attendance on committee meetings, the
president should take pains not to usurp the place
of the chairman.   Though he may occasionally give
hints to the entire committee, it is much better to suggest plans in private to the chairman, and, if possible,
make him think that they are *his* plans.   The chairman will then be more interested in carrying them
out. The president, therefore, should not talk much
at the committee meeting—just a word here and
there, when it is needed ; and especially let him be
lavish of praise, encouragement, and good cheer.
He should hold in memory his own beginnings in
committee work, remember his mistakes, and recall
how much good such kindness from the president
would have done him at that time.

When the president finds it especially difficult to
go to the committee meetings, he may adopt a plan
whose very novelty will render it even more effect-
ive than his visits—he may send them a letter to
be read at the meeting,—a letter of warm, Christian brotherhood, commending them for all their
good work, and telling them of something he would
like to have them do.

The best thing the president can do for a committee is to use it.   He should never do himself what he can get a committee to do for him.

At the opening of his term of office, the president should have a clear idea of what he wants from each committee—some step in advance for the committee as a whole and as individual members.   Tell them of it, and hold them up to it.   Give each committee a year's motto embodying your ambition for it. The giving of these mottoes will of itself make a pretty exercise for some meeting at the beginning of the term.   Keep your eye on each committee, and see that they all are at work.   One page of a special note-book should be given up to each committee, and filled with brief notes regarding its plans and progress, together with new methods that may be suggested to them.

The president can do his committees a service by talking with other presidents about their committees, and reporting to his own society whatever methods he may thus learn.   By all means see that your committees attend the committee conferences of your local union, take part themselves, and carry away as many good notions as possible.   Put them in touch also with the best committee helps, introducing them to the price-list of the United Society of Christian Endeavor publications.

It is the custom of some societies, and might well become the custom in all societies, to appoint every member to some committee, and even when new members join in the course of a year, the president publicly assigns them to some committee as so on as their names appear on the society's roll.   If a chairmanship lapses, the president should at once see that it is filled by a nomination from the executive committee (unless your constitution provides some other way), and by the election of the society.

Of course this patient, careful, vigorous oversight of the committees will not need to be lavished upon all of them equally. There will be many committees, and possibly the majority of them, led by skilled workers, whose labors will move with sufficient smoothness and force without his aid, so that he can largely concentrate his efforts upon the few committees that are weak and inexperienced. In helping them he will be doing most fruitful service, he will be training up laborers for the vineyard of his Master.

CHAPTER VII.

THE PRESIDENT AND THE UNIONS.

IN probably a large majority of our city and county or district Christian Endeavor unions, the president is a member of the executive committee. By virtue of this office he is presumably well informed regarding union matters, and it is through his interest that the society is likely to be kept in touch with the union. How important this is, it ought not to be necessary to explain. Christian Endeavor exists not alone for the local society, nor even for the local church with which it is connected, but for all the brotherhood of churches. One of the special advantages of the Endeavor movement is the fact that it is interdenominational, and this side of its work is best brought out in the local union. A society that has nothing to do with its local union is quite certain to be of little benefit to its church and its own members, because it will lack the enthusiasm that comes from numbers and the knowledge that it is a part of the mighty army, and it will not share in the free interchange of new methods which adds to each society in the union the wisdom and practical experience of all. An isolated society is only half a society.

Of course, if the president is to arouse in his society an enthusiasm for the union, he must attend

faithfully the union executive committee neetings.
For the honor of the society which he represents, as
well as for the sake of thē great cause in which the
union is at work, let him go to these meetings with
his head full of new ideas. In my manual, "Our
Unions," I have treated union work with fulness in
all its branches, and society presidents may be glad
to know about the little book. Our president should
be ready to take part in the discussions, tell the experience of his society whenever that experience is
called for or would be helpful, give his opinion on
all points with modesty yet with force, and in every
way uphold the hands of the union officers and show
that his Endeavorers are willing to do their full duty.
If speakers are needed for any exercise, he should
mention those in his society or church that might
perform the duty acceptably. If a sum of money
must be raised for the union work, he should be
bold enough to pledge his society to help, and he
may even name the sum, it being understood that
his society must vote on the matter. If a place for
the next meeting is needed, let him offer his own
church, having previously won permission from the
proper authorities.

It is usually the president that has to announce
before his society the next meeting of the union.
There are several ways of doing this. One is the
scolding way, which says, in effect: "There were
not half as many of you at the last union meeting as
should have been there, and I am ashamed of you."
Another is the stupid way, reading hastily in a half-
audible tone the notice (often a card, and needing

to be expanded) of the union secretary. Another is
the scattering way, which talks long and tediously
about non-essentials, and leaves out of the notice
almost everything that people want to know. The
right way to announce the union meeting is not to
read, but to give the information in your own words;
to speak with earnestness, as if you meant what you
said ; to speak brightly, putting a little fun into it ;
to be business-like, making it very clear just who is
to speak, where the meeting is to be held, and just
when it will begin. This notice should be given as
early as possible, with a request that the members
reserve the evening of the meeting ; then let it be
repeated on each succeeding week. The giving of
notices in such a way that they will be heeded, and
so attractively as to make people want to attend the
meeting, is really a fine art. It cannot be done off-
hand. It needs preparation as much as anything in
the meeting. The society should have a bulletin
board,—it will prove of value in a great many unexpected ways. The secretary's notice should be
posted upon this board, together with whatever else
may arouse interest in the coming union gathering.

The best way to make sure of a good attendance
at the meetings of the union is for the president to
constitute himself a committee of one to see every
member and urge him to go. Let the members go
in a body. Charter an electric car. Agree to meet
on a certain train. Sit together at the union meeting. Applaud in a solid phalanx. Carry your society banner. Wear your society badges. A society
cannot do good work without a strong, hearty *esprit*

de corps, and the union meetings afford an unequal-
ed opportunity for the cultivation of that spirit.

It is the president's business also to see that his
society has its full share in the activities of the union
that may not be quite so public. For instance, when
the union holds a committee conference, he should
make sure that his own society sends its committee,
—entire, if possible. If the union carries on a press
department, he should see that his own society and
church report their work with brightness and regularity. He will interest himself in the prompt response to all requests for statistics from the union
secretary, and for money from the union treasurer.
The expenses of a Christian Endeavor union are so
slight that no society should be remiss in contribut-
ing its small share. If the union officers do not of
their own accord visit his society, our model president will give them a cordial invitation, and when
any one of them comes, the president will give him
a warm introduction to the society, ask him to
speak, and thank him heartily at the close, getting
up a little reception for him at the end of the meeting.

Much of what has been said with reference to the
local union will apply to the State union and the
United Society of Christian Endeavor, with the conventions held by these bodies. It is by the president
naturally that the society will be interested in these
important bodies and assemblies—an interest which
bears rich fruit, not only in the society, but in the
great work at large.

CHAPTER VIII.

THE WORK OF THE VICE-PRESIDENT.

IF any officer has need to magnify his office, it is the vice-president. From the vice-president of the United States down, this office is held to be almost a sinecure, with little responsibility and therefore little honor. Let it not be so in our Christian Endeavor societies.

For to neglect the possibilities of the vice-president is not only to suggest inaction to one who is probably among your best workers, but it is to rob your president of much of his efficiency, and the society of one of its leaders. The vice-president should be not only a substitute for the president when he is away, but the president's right hand when he is at-home. The very fact that the vice-president will be obliged in the absence of the president to do all his work for him is enough to hint pretty broadly at the wisdom of giving the vice-president some of that work to do before the entire responsibility is thrust upon him.

A president is indeed foolish if, having furnished him by the society an officer especially for his assistance—a favor granted to no other officer of the society—he disregards his vice-president, and carries on his work unaided. It is hard to say who is most injured by such a course—the president, the vice-president, or the society.

In some societies the vice-president is chosen with as much care as the president, because in those societies it is the custom to elevate the vice-president the next term to the presidency. The plan has much to recommend it. It provides for president some one that has already passed a capital apprenticeship in the duties of his office, and certainly the office of vice-president in such a society is no sinecure, no empty honor.

In other societies it is the custom to make the vice-president the chairman *ex officio* of the most important Christian Endeavor committee—the lookout committee. Thus he is given work to do, and at the same time is at hand ready for the president's absence. I do not myself think this plan quite as good as the one just mentioned.

In any event, the vice-president should be the president's right-hand man. Certain definite responsibilities should be thrown upon him, and if the president does not do this, the vice-president may well offer to assume them. For instance, since the president is supposed to oversee the work of all the committees, occasionally being present at their meetings, spurring the sluggish, praising the zealous, advising the inexperienced,—a share in this difficult and arduous work should be given to the vice-president, perhaps half of the committees being placed in his care. He should always be present at the meetings of the executive committee, and sometimes the president should get him to preside at those meetings, and also at the regular society business meetings even when the president himself is there. On other occasions the president may entrust to the vice-president the presentation of certain matters of business; and in the prayer meetings, when announcements must be made, let the president not make them always himself, but sometimes ask the vice-president to make them. The president will often refer to the vice-president in speaking to the society, recognizing the work he is doing, and bringing his office to the attention of the members.

As for the rest of the vice-president's work, the ground is covered, of course, in the chapters on the president, since he is simply to be the president's helper, and to learn all he can about the president's business, in order that he may be ready to step right into the president's place when that officer is called away. To those chapters, therefore, I refer the vice-presidents who read this book.

CHAPTER IX.

THE RECORDING SECRETARY'S WORK.

ALAS for the society that is burdened with the fussy secretary, or the untidy secretary, or the inac-curate secretary, or the slow secretary, or the timid secretary, or the giggling secretary, or any other kind of secretary but the right kind ! The secretary has much to do with the success of two meetings every month—the business meeting and the con-secration meeting, and with many important society interests during the intervening time. But her work (it usually is *hers* and not *his*) is not difficult or complicated ; and if it is done promptly, it takes but little time.

In the first place, as to the minutes of the society, they should be kept neatly, in a substantial book solely for that purpose. Fine penmanship is not essential, and, indeed, " copybook " penmanship is usually very hard to read ; but distinct penmanship is essential. Of importance, too, is attention to spelling, and the knowledge that paragraphs must begin some distance in from the margin. Black ink, jet black, should always be used, since you want to make a permanent record.

The minutes should include all motions passed, using the same words in which the motion is put by the president. If you are in doubt, get it written out for you. Shorthand is of much assistance to a secretary. Do not, however, needlessly delay the meeting to obtain the exact wording of unimportant resolutions, but only of those where the identical wording is likely to come in question later.

Often, moreover, it is well for the secretary to record the motions that fail to pass, since frequently refusal to take action is of much significance. In general, all important business, whether positive or negative in its nature, should be recorded. I myself like the custom of recording also the names of all makers of motions, as I believe that this little piece of recognition tends to increase the interest of the members in the society business.

Do not take notes carelessly. In the course of the business meeting a secretary is often called upon to state just what motion has been passed at an earlier part of the meeting, and should be ready to turn at once to the motion and read it exactly. Learn to write out the minutes during the discussions.

Do not put off transcribing the notes you have taken, but write them at once before they get "cold." The work will be far easier and more accurate if it is done promptly. Do not let your minutes be wordy; a brisk, business-like style shown in the minutes read at the opening of the business meeting seems always to add to the briskness of the meeting. Have regard also to the literary quality of your records. Get rid of awkward expressions. Seek for neat turns of words. They must be accurate, of course; but if to your accuracy you add earnestness, your minutes will uplift the society; and if to your earnestness you add a bit of spice, you will win and hold attention, without which no amount of earnestness produces much result. I propose, then, three " f's " for your minutes: fact, fun, and force.

Do not mind it if your minutes are criticised when the president calls for corrections, but receive the emendations with Christian humility. Never copy the minutes into the record book until they have been approved.

Become familiar with the minutes of former years, since there is no knowing when some member of the society may wish for information in the business meetings, or elsewhere, on what the society has already done in regard to almost any subject. Take the book with you to all meetings of the society, and also the book containing the membership roll. You will often find occasion to use both.

It is your duty, unless there is a society library, to preserve carefully the old record books of the society. These volumes, you must not forget, contain all the society history there is. Some secretaries do a useful and pleasant thing for the society by getting up a card catalogue of society members, old and new, each card containing a condensed history of the member—his birthplace, the date when he joined the society, his full address, and the like. When members graduate, or move away, the secretary still keeps track of them, and adds the chief facts that come to her knowledge, such as their marriage or entrance upon some important undertaking. In future years such a card catalogue is invaluable for reference.

It is the secretary's duty—again in case there is no society library—to receive and preserve all the committee reports. To this end they should be written on uniform paper, which the society might well furnish, and the reports of one year should be bound together, unless you prefer to place in patent "binders" the reports of the several committees by themselves, so that each committee can at any time examine the history of all work along its line done in the society during the past years. If you follow this excellent plan, the secretary should still have the custody of the reports, but she should hand each file to the proper committee early in the term, so that the chairman may read it through.

If the president and the society do not insist upon written reports, nevertheless the secretary should insist, and she should urge their value and necessity until this most beneficial custom has become established.

The secretary's own report at the business meeting should be a general review of the month's work—a sort of condensation of her executive committee minutes. For the secretary should always attend the executive committee meetings, and should act as the committee's secretary, keeping its minutes as carefully as those of the society itself, since the executive committee is more of a deliberative body than the society. In addition, of course, she should feel free to make suggestions at any time, and, indeed, to take as full part in the executive com-

5

mittee meetings as any of the committee chairmen.

Another very important duty of the secretary is
the calling of the roll at the consecration meeting,
though a few societies assign this task to the leader
for the evening, and a few give it to the president.
Much of the success of this meeting depends upon
the way in which the roll is called. A poky secretary, with a low, mumbling voice, can spoil the
effect of the best consecration service, while a secretary with a clear, loud voice, brisk, business-like,
and happy, infuses life into the meeting with every
name she calls. She should sit in front, facing the
society, so that she can see who is present, and not
linger over the names of the absent except long
enough to permit the reading of a message if any
has been sent. If the leader does not interrupt the
roll-call at intervals by announcing a hymn, the
secretary should do that herself. When she comes
to her own name, she should read it, and follow it
with her own testimony. It is better, in my judgment, always to say "Mr." and "Miss" with the
names.

There are different ways of calling the roll, and
the use of variety in this exercise will free the consecration service from any danger of monotony.
The leader may arrange for the variation, but if he
does not, the secretary has a perfect right to do so.
Try calling the names in the reverse order, beginning at the end of the alphabet. Again, call the letters of the alphabet, "A " first, whereupon all whose
names begin with A will take part, the secretary

noting who speaks ; then B, and so on. Try placing upon a blackboard the list of members, who will speak without any roll-call at all, the secretary making the record silently. Try calling the names in a hit-or-miss way, so that no member will know when he is to be called upon. Sometimes call the names of the committees, and as each committee is called, its members will rise and speak in the order in which they stand, its chairman closing with a prayer for the committee. Try a "voluntary" consecration meeting, the first part of the evening being given up to voluntary participation, at the close of which the roll is called, those that have already spoken responding merely with "present." There are many other ways of varying the consecration meetings, and for a full account of them I must refer secretaries to my pamphlet on the consecration meeting, "Our Crowning Meeting," which is published by the United Society of Christian Endeavor (ten cents).

The membership roll of the society should be kept by the secretary in a book by itself, at the opening of which is the constitution. There should be separate sections of the book for the active, associate, and honorary members. It is the secretary's business to see that each newly elected member signs the constitution, and also that he signs a copy of the pledge, which he retains to be put in some place where it will serve as a constant reminder of his vows. It is very necessary that the membership lists should be kept accurately and up to date. The secretary should never add or remove a name without proper authority,—namely, that of the lookout committee. It is not within the province of the secretary to transfer a member at his request to the much-abused "absent members' list." No change whatever should be made in the list without the vote of the lookout committee and the pastor.

Only two points more, and the secretary's work will have been outlined. He should notify all committees of their appointment, and all officers of their election, and this notification should be in writing. He ranks next to the president and the vice-president, and will be the proper presiding officer in case neither of these others is present. In that case, the secretary calls the meeting to order, asks that a chairman of the meeting be nominated, puts the vote, and then returns to the secretary's desk, leaving the president's chair to the temporary substitute.

CHAPTER X.

THE CORRESPONDING SECRETARY'S WORK.

THE corresponding secretary is unique among Christian Endeavor officers in that his office is permanent. With the officers changing every year, and in many societies twice a year, a permanent secretary is a necessity in order that the United Society and the State and local unions may keep in touch with the local societies. These could not recast their lists continually to insert the names of newly chosen officers, nor is it likely that the new officers would often be reported to headquarters.

Just because of his permanency, however, the corresponding secretary is more likely than any other officer to become "dead wood," to lose his interest and fail to do his duty. Then we have confusion indeed. Then the United Society and the State and local union find it impossible to gather the most important statistics. Then the most important communications — communications absolutely necessary for the success of the movement at large and the inspiration of the society's work—fail to get further than the corresponding secretary's overcoat pocket. Then, the link being broken, the society is cut off from its connection with the rest of the Christian Endeavor world.

So let it be distinctly understood that the corresponding secretary is a permanent officer only so long as he takes active interest in the society and does his work faithfully. It is not hard work, and it is little to ask of him; he is inexcusable if he does not keep it up, and has no right to feel hurt if he is quietly dropped and another Endeavorer put in his place. To facilitate such a change, when it is necessary, always nominate and elect the corresponding secretary with the rest of the officers, though the same person is chosen term after term. When a new corresponding secretary is elected, be sure to send his name to the General Secretary of the United Society, and to the secretaries of your State, county or district, and city unions.

As already indicated, the corresponding secretary's main duty is simply to receive and pass along whatever communications may be sent to the society. It is not his business to sift them, but to hand them all to the president or the recording secretary of the society, for presentation at the executive committee meeting, or for direct presentation to the society, as the case may be. There are, however, certain documents with which the society should have nothing to do, and as the corresponding secretary is likely to be more experienced than any other officer, in passing these along he should give his judgment upon them, and advise that no attention be paid to them. For instance, letters will come from persons who wish to enlist the Endeavorers in various enterprises that are entirely outside of legitimate Christian Endeavor work. These usually call for money, that should be given to the church and denomination with which the society is connected. Some struggling church out West may be trying to pay off its debt, and "ten cents from every Christian Endeavor society" will do it, oh, so easily! (I should think it would!) Or some enthusiast may take it into his head that all the young people of the State should support a Christian Endeavor missionary, and send out circulars for that purpose, quite oblivious of the fact that Christian Endeavor belongs to many denominations, while the missionary of necessity would belong to only one. Such wild schemes are proposed to every church organization; there is not a pastor who has not his pocket full of such letters all the time. When they come to the corresponding secretary, it is his business to see that they are *not* acted on. The United Society of Christian Endeavor will send once a year a request for statistics. It never asks for money, nor receives a cent of contributions from any society. It is supported entirely by its publication department and by the Christian Endeavor organ, *The Christian Endeavor World.* The officers of your State and city Christian Endeavor union will send occasional communications suggesting ways of working, seeking to inspire you to better activities, advertising the State convention and the local-union meetings, and perhaps calling for a dollar or two—never for more—in support of the interdenominational work of Christian Endeavor. These communications should be passed promptly to the proper officer—usually the president. You will often receive word from your denominational authorities,

and especially the missionary boards and the denominational periodicals. These circulars will be
given all possible attention. As each is received,
say to yourself, "The King's business requireth
haste." In fine, whatever bears upon it the legitimate Christian Endeavor or denominational stamp,
you are to send at once along the channel of usefulness. If at any time you are in doubt as to the disposition of part of your mail, carry it at once to
your pastor, or ask the president to do so. He has
the right to say what subjects and appeals should be
brought before his Christian Endeavor society.

It is best for the corresponding secretary to make
it a rule never to reply to letters received, unless definitely instructed to do so by the executive committee. Of course, a mere call for statistics from the
proper source should be answered without troubling
the executive committee with it. The corresponding secretary will need here the help of the recording secretary. But he should answer no letters from
unauthorized persons—those, for instance, that wish
the names of the Endeavorers for advertising purposes.

It will often be the duty of the corresponding secretary to present to the society, when directed to do
so by the president, the contents of circulars and
letters that he has received. It may be, for instance,
an appeal for money made by the home missionary
board of your denomination. Don't be satisfied with
a dry and lifeless reading of the circular. Remember: you are, for the time being, the proxy of that
great missionary society. Study the matter, become

filled with facts, make the appeal in your own words and as if you were a lawyer addressing a jury in a case where life is at stake.

Finally, it is often the duty of the corresponding secretary to correspond, himself, as well as receive the correspondence of others. If a member of the society is moving to another town, and wishes a letter of introduction to the society there, it is his duty to give it, on direction of the executive committee. If, as sometimes happens—not so often, however, as might be to advantage—there comes from some distant society a request for an interchange of methods along some line of Christian Endeavor work, he is the one who should reply, and his letter should be crammed with practical helpfulness and cordial Christian brotherliness. It is a genuine missionary service to write such letters, and correspondence of this character, inspiring and fruitful in the highest degree, might well be initiated by any corresponding secretary.

But there is a work akin to this that is even more important, and that is sending items of interest to the international Christian Endeavor organ, *The Christian Endeavor World,* and to the papers of your own denomination. The editors of these papers are always eager for such items, provided—and this is an important *if*—they are of general interest and importance. A list of your new officers is of no importance to the outside world. Even a notice of that noble young woman who has just died and left your society desolate would not interest other societies, unless there is some striking and unusual

fact to tell, since this is, alas! so common an occur-
rence. But if you have originated some new plan
of work or if in some fresh way you have carried
out some old plan, if to some notable degree God's
Spirit has been working in your midst, leading young
hearts to Himself, if you are doing large things for
the mission boards, if you have held a unique social,
if you are helping your pastor in some novel way—
if, in short, any of your endeavors will, in your
opinion, be worth the attention of the larger world,
then it is more than your privilege, it is your duty,
to pass it on. That is one of the reasons why you
belong to an interdenominational movement—because you believe in the widest possible helpfulness.
Don't tell your story at great length. Leave out the
proper names. Give the essentials, and omit the
non-essentials. When you have written a page,
write it once more in half a page, and then don't be
grieved if the unfeeling editor cuts it down to two
sentences. Remember, there are other societies, and
other corresponding secretaries, and other Endeavorers, who also are doing things.

CHAPTER XI.

THE TREASURER'S WORK.

IT is no unimportant business to be set over the King's treasury, even a small branch of it. Our Christian Endeavor treasurers, if they will magnify their office, may have much to do in training up a generation of generous, systematic givers. The little sums they will receive are therefore more than they seem ; they are earnests of far greater sums the church will receive in the coming years as the result of this faithful service.

The Christian Endeavor treasurer, then, should be an enthusiast in the finances of the kingdom. He should be a young " Napoleon of finance " for the kingdom of heaven. He should not be afraid to talk dollars, or ashamed to ask for money in a good cause. He should be a good giver himself, that he may ask with a good countenance. He should be patient, energetic, orderly, prompt, faithful. These are the exemplary treasurer's qualities.

The treasurer's labors resolve themselves into three parts: getting the money, recording it, and paying it out.

The first part is the most important and difficult. The only plan for raising money that I can recommend is the pledge-envelope system. At the opening of the society year, the treasurer presents to each Endeavorer a card headed :

"For the expenses of the Christian Endeavor society, and for its gifts to missions, I promise to pay this year, monthly, the sum that is checked below. This pledge may be withdrawn by notice to the treasurer.

1 cent.............................
2 cents.... ....,
3 cents.............................
4 cents ... .
5 cents.............................
10 cents.............................
25 cents ....
50 cents ....
(Date)............ (Signature)..............

Some societies will prefer to put more figures in the list between five and twenty-five. These cards may be worked off on a manifolding machine, or they may be purchased from the United Society of Christian Endeavor. Just before they are given out to the members, the treasurer should say a word to the society, emphasizing the facts that small gifts become big ones if many are added together, that it is especially necessary for the society to train its members in giving, that *every* member should contribute something, no matter how little, that no one but the treasurer will know how much each person contributes, and that, while no one should stop short of the largest gift he can rightfully make, yet all should remember that what God wants is the spirit of giving, and that He was as well pleased with the widow's mite as with any gift ever made by a millionaire.

It is well to announce at this time for just what purposes the money received is to be used. Make this plain, because no one likes to give without knowing for what he is giving. The executive committee should consider the matter with care, and present a plan to the society for adoption. Of course, unless you have a more distinct idea of what will be contributed than most societies have, you can deal only in proportions, not in amounts. You might propose to the society, for instance, that of the sums received each month one-fourth be set aside for society expenses, and three-fourths for missions. Unless the church needs some of the money, the latter fund should be divided equally— three-eighths to home, and three-eighths to foreign, missions. I believe, too, that it is most advantageous to fix upon the objects of your gifts as early in the year as possible—just what boards, and missions, and schools, and persons you will give to, if your boards permit such definite giving. Of course, you should leave some lee-way for unexpected calls to which you may want to respond, but you will miss many noble opportunities of interesting the society in missions, if you do not know through the year pretty definitely where your money is going.

As the pledge cards come in, give to each Endeavorer a bundle of twelve little envelopes, to be obtained from the United Society of Christian Endeavor. These envelopes will bear upon them the names of the mouths of the year, and also a number by which the Endeavorer is known upon the treasurer's books, and by which his gift is identified in the collection when it is received.

The monthly offerings should be made at the consecration meeting. That is the appropriate time, since it is the consecration of your money as well as the rest of yourself and your belongings that is to be emphasized. It should come at the beginning of the consecration meeting, and might well be preceded by a brief prayer. The president or the leader will make the announcement and appoint members to "take up the collection," or this duty may be imposed upon the treasurer.

The record of each member, according to this system, should be kept separately, but the whole is very quickly done if you have a large sheet of paper bearing a vertical list of the names, and after each name twelve spaces. The names are numbered, and as each envelope is opened its contents is noted in the proper place opposite the name bearing its number. I believe that a treasurer should receipt for everything, if he would get the best results in the way of giving, and so I should even receipt for each of these monthly gifts. Let it be understood that the return of the envelope, bearing the giver's name in the treasurer's handwriting, constitutes the receipt for each month.

Emphasize the importance of giving these sums, though they are small, *every month*, rather than wait and let them accumulate. Never hesitate to inform delinquents that they are behindhand. Not every month, possibly, but still frequently, it is best for the treasurer to report to the society, in general terms, how the society finances stand, and how many pledges remain unpaid.

This business-like plan is far superior to a collection taken spasmodically. It is infinitely superior to the plan of raising money by "pay socials." It is sometimes wise to add to your missionary fund, or raise money for special purposes, by such means as a lecture course or a concert; but such entertainments should never be the main dependence. The only way to give is—to give!

I thoroughly believe, however, in special collections. They are a sort of "free-will offerings" of the kind so widely used in the old Jewish days. An especially helpful custom is the "self-denial week" preceding the annual celebration of Christian Endeavor Day, resulting in a grand "thank-offering" on our anniversary. This thank-offering is almost always distributed equally between home and foreign missions.

Some societies have found it a good plan to stimulate sluggish giving by taking a collection at *every* meeting, not pledging the members as to the amounts, but earnestly asking that *each* member shall bring *something*, however small the amount, *every week.*

It is a part of the treasurer's duties to promote more generous giving,—of course in conjunction each time with other officers and committees, if the enterprise lies in the line of their work. An occasional diagram may be devised, to be hung on the wall. For instance, he may draw cubes representing by their relative sizes the payments of the average Christian for missions, for clothes, for food, for soda-water, and the like. The Tenth Legion—our Christian Endeavor organization for tithe-givers, and the Macedonian Phalanx—the Christian Endeavor movement to promote giving to definite missionary objects, may be pushed by no Endeavorer so appropriately as the treasurer. Material for advertising these movements may be obtained from the United Society of Christian Endeavor.

The treasurer's account-book should be neatly kept. It is especially necessary, if he would not get into a muddle, that every receipt and expenditure be recorded *immediately*. He should give a receipt for everything, using a regular printed receipt book, or printing blanks upon a manifolder:

.... (Place and date)
Received from   ...., ... dollars and .... cents for...........................
On behalf of the ...... Christian Endeavor Society, ..., *Treasurer.*

He should be equally particular in requiring vouchers for every cent he gives out—from committee chairmen, speakers, mission boards, and every one. A regular printed receipt book may be bought for a little, or vouchers may be printed on the society manifolder:

.... (Place and date)
Received from .... , Treasurer of the.......
Christian Endeavor Society, ... dollars and .....
cents, for ....-...
(Signature) ....
(Official position) ....

If the pledge system is used, as I have described it, the treasurer will open up an account with each member of the society, though for simplicity's sake this pledge account may be condensed upon a very few pages. There should also be separate page accounts with each committee that draws money from the treasury, with home and foreign missions, and the like. Head the left-hand page "Dr." and the right-hand page "Cr.," writing in the center the person or cause or committee with whom you are accounting. The full form would be, " I, the treasurer (understood) am debtor to—(the social committee, say), in the following appropriation made for the use of that committee by the society, and creditor by the following sums paid to the chairman of that committee." Precede the items on the debit side by the preposition " to," and on the credit side by the preposition " by."

A simpler form of account will record on the debit side of the ledger whatever sums have been received, with the date in each case and the source, and on the credit side whatever sums have been paid out, with the date and the object or person receiving them.

No money should be paid out for any purpose without express authorization from the executive committee or vote of the society. In some societies it is required that the secretary write an order upon the treasurer for each sum so voted, the treasurer keeping that order as his authorization for the expenditure; but usually that is an unnecessary form in a Christian Endeavor society, since the treasurer

6

will be in attendance always upon the meetings of the executive committee and the business meetings of the society. Payments to the missionary boards should always be sent to the treasurers of those boards, and they may be sent direct or through the church treasurer, according to the preference of the church. When the church treasurer sends them, he should give a receipt to the Christian Endeavor treasurer ; and in either case, when the gift is sent, the mission board should be asked to note that the money comes from the Christian Endeavor society. Most boards keep a special record of the gifts from Christian Endeavor societies, just as they keep a special record of the gifts from Sunday schools.

The treasurer's report should be given at each business meeting, that the society may always know just how it stands financially. How much detail is to be introduced depends on the need of the society and on the amount and complexity of the society's business. It is profitless, for instance, to tell what the social committee paid out for lemonade, but it may be useful for the society to know how much their topic cards cost, and all gifts to missions should be given with full particulars. Figures may easily be made very dry, or, with the exercise of some pains and ingenuity, they may be made very interesting. If the treasurer is bright, his report may be one of the best and most inspiring features of the business meeting. Put it as little as possible in tabular form, and as much as possible in narrative form. Mass the details so that they may readily be grasped, and print the more significant facts upon a blackboard or a large sheet of paper, that the impetus of generous giving may enter through Eye-gate as well as Ear-gate. Be as enterprising as an advertising agent,—I can give no more emphatic comparison,—for is it not the King's business that you are promoting?

CHAPTER XII.

THE ORGANIST'S WORK.

WHEN it is remembered how much of the brightness and attractiveness of our prayer meetings come
from the singing, and how far the singing is influ-
enced by a good accompanist, or the reverse, it will
be seen why I consider the organist one of the most
important of Christian Endeavor officers. A large
part of the success of every prayer meeting depends
on her. If she enters into her work with enthusiasm and skill, and with the higher motive of desire
to further Christ's cause, and not the low motive of
love for music, or the still lower motive, the wish to
show off, then the members will be likely to "sing
with grace in their hearts unto the Lord." Such
singing will render every member more zealous in
his Christian endeavors, and, best of all, souls will
be won by it for the kingdom of God.

In some societies the music committee chooses the
organist; in others, this officer is elected with the
others. I prefer the latter method, provided you are
careful to pass the work around in turn to all that
can do it well. Now and then put a beginner in
this place, remembering that our society is to be
first and always a training school for service.
In my own society we had at one time no fewer

than six organists, each serving for a month at a time.

It is especially necessary that you organists should be promptly in your place at the beginning of the meeting, as soon as the leader has taken the chair. Have the book open before you. Most meetings begin with a song, so that you, even more than the leader, give the meeting its initial impetus upon which so much depends.

Find the page quickly, and be sure you get the right one. If you are in doubt what hymn is called for at any time during the meeting, do not hesitate to ask, rather than guess at it. Remember, if you failed to hear, doubtless the others are in the same predicament. If at any time you hear the number yourself, but judge that others may not have heard, repeat it in a distinct voice.

Notice carefully what verses are to be omitted in singing. How often have we seen a careless organist start out confidently on another verse after the last stanza had already been sung, play a few measures, and then stop in confusion amid the titters of the irreverent! That is always a hurt to the meeting.

If you perceive that the society has become con·· fused, and that half of them are singing the wrong verse, do not hesitate at the beginning of the next stanza to call its number clearly. Whether you will do such things, or not, will depend of course upon whether there is in the chair a leader who will do them.

Unless the song is one quite unknown to the

society, do not play it all through as a prelude. This custom is a great nuisance in many societies, and constitutes more of a drag than is commonly realized. A few measures will be sufficient, just to be certain that every one has found the place; then sound the key-note and enter at once upon the song.

The same remarks apply even more emphatically to interludes. In most cases they are mere impertinences, and serve only to impede the swing of the music, and make a needless break in our appreciation of the thoughts of the hymn. If the hymn is a long one, a very brief interlude toward the close may be needed in order to get breath; but for a hymn of the ordinary length it is quite unnecessary. Make a slight pause after each stanza, then strike the key-note firmly, and begin at once with decision the next verse.

Do not leave the organ during the meeting, unless sitting on a stool without a back is very wearisome. The time occupied in taking your place is lost to the meeting, and your moving about makes always more or less of a disturbance. Hold yourself in instant readiness for any musical demand.

Sing, if you can, and as strongly as possible. You are the natural leader of the music, by voice as well as with the instrument. And you will do the society an especial benefit if now and then you start up some appropriate hymn without announcement of any kind. Of course the hymn should be sufficiently familiar for the Endeavorers to join you without having recourse to their books, and this feature will add much to the vivacity and interest of the meeting.

For this purpose, and for many other purposes, it will be a great advantage to you if you will commit tunes to memory—as many of the common tunes as possible. That will give you facility in playing, enable you to exchange a poor tune for a good one when certain words are desired, conduct "sings" where books are not available, and in many other ways make yourself a musical blessing.

Of course, whether you commit the tunes to memory or not, you will become familiar with them all, so that no one can catch you by calling for a tune you cannot readily play. That the society also may have this familiarity, you will do a good deed if you organize little meetings for practice of the less known hymns, holding the gatherings at your own house.

Such work should be done by the music committee, if you have one ; and if you have none, you are the fit person to see that this useful committee is added to your society's complement of tools. And, by the way, you will find in my manual for music committees, "Christian Endeavor Grace-Notes," published by the United Society of Christian Endeavor (10 cents), a large number of plans and suggestions that will aid you in your work.

Note the character of each piece before you play it, and try to make your playing harmonize with the sentiment. Do not rattle off "Nearer, my God, to Thee" as if it were "Captain Jinks," nor prolong

"Onward, Christian soldiers" as if it were "Poor old Pidy, she died last Friday."

It is unnecessary, of course, to say, "Don't drag." No organist ever *did* drag knowingly, though I have suffered under organists that were so sure they were not dragging that they paid no heed to their audience, and came out half a mile behind.

It is far more necessary to say, in writing for young musicians especially, "Don't race ahead." You may be conscious that the society are dragging fearfully, but hammering angrily on the instrument is no way to bring them to time; it only advertises your temper. If you find that, on your keeping just a trifle ahead of the members, they do not take the hint and catch up, speak a word about it in public, or, better, talk the matter over in private with the leading singers.

Do not convert the prayer meeting into a singing school. It is never wise to stop a hymn in order to tell how it should be sung. Do not give folks the impression that you mind a false note more than a false spirit.

A knowledge of harmony, and the ability to change the key so as bring the music more easily within the range of the members' voices, will help you greatly in your work, though of course it is not at all essential.

Do not let your position as organist excuse you from testifying in every meeting. The very conspicuousness of your post makes it necessary for you to testify for the sake of the example, if for no other reason.

And put religion into all your musical work. Get in touch with the Master, if you want a beautiful " touch " on your instrument. Get a love for this noble task and an enthusiasm for it, and believe in it with all your soul. In a very real way you are helping to preach the gospel.

CHAPTER XIII.

THE EXECUTIVE COMMITTEE.

You will have a good society if you have good executive committee meetings. No other committee is so important, because this is the co-ordinating and the focusing committee. It sets the society to work, and keeps it at work. It discovers flaws, and remedies them. It discovers excellencies, and praises them. It is the pastor's cabinet among the young people, and an hour here once a month will enable him to accomplish more than ten times an hour spent in any other way. It is also the president's chance at the leaders of the society, and if his touch here is firm and sure, he can mold the society to his desire. It is the committees' chance at one another, so that whatever aid one committee wants from the other members, it will here apply for, and whatever suggestion it has for the good of the society, it will here bring to a head. If the lookout committee are the society's eyes, and the prayer-meeting committee its heart, the executive committee make up its brain, where all nerves center, and from which all active impulses properly come forth.

The committee is made up of the chairmen of all the committees, together with all the officers. Do not forget the vice-president. Sometimes let him preside, even when the president is there. This will render him more interested in the meetings of the committee, and will train him for an emergency and also to become president himself by and by. Do not forget the corresponding secretary, either,— an officer most necessary to have at the meetings, but often left out. The recording secretary should be there, of course, and should act as the secretary of the committee. The Junior superintendent should be present to report for that important branch of the work, and receive help from the other Endeavorers. I should even have the organist there, once in a while at least, and when she is present, make it a point to talk over the music of the society. The treasurer should never be absent, since questions of finance are likely to be involved in all kinds of committee work. Certainly the pastor should be present whenever this is feasible, and every wide-awake pastor will be glad of the privilege.

The presiding officer, of course, is the president, and he will hold the committee to as strict rules of procedure as the regular business meeting of the society. A committee meeting is so informal in its appearance that unless it is held in check with a strong hand, it is likely to fritter itself away in pleasant but aimless and fruitless chat.

As to the time for the meeting, once a month is often enough, unless for special reasons an extra session is needed. The meeting should precede the monthly business meeting of the society, because one of the chief duties of the executive committee is to sift out the business, and discuss it, and put it in such shape that the society can act upon it speedily and with little need for any debate, thus saving time for the more strictly religious exercises. But be sure to hold the meeting three or four days before the business meeting, since points may come up in the committee meeting that will need several days to be put into proper shape for the society. Have a regular day of the week for the meeting, and vary from it only when you really must. It is a great aid to memory to hold committee meetings always on the same date.

For the same reason have, if possible, a regular place for the meeting, and a private house is better for the purpose—far better—than the church. Let it be the same house always, and, if convenient, the president's house.

Begin promptly at the fixed time, though only a portion of the committee are present. To wait for the late comers will only perpetuate the nuisance of their tardiness, whereas if they learn that you will begin on time, they will get there on time themselves—possibly.

Open the meeting with prayer. Sometimes the president may offer this prayer, or ask some one else to offer it, or call for two or three prayers in succession. Thus you will get into the right spirit at the very start.

Call next for the reading of the minutes of the last meeting. The secretary should keep these minutes as carefully as those of the business meeting, but in a separate book. Never omit the reading of the minutes, since that will recall to mind what was done at the last meeting, and will remind you of many points upon which reports at this meeting will be in order.

Next, the president will ask each chairman in turn to report for his line of work. In some societies there are read at the executive committee meeting the reports that are to be presented to the society at the coming business meeting. They are read here in order that the entire committee may criticise them, suggesting corrections, omissions, or additions; and the custom is a good one.

A good committee report contains four elements; it should tell (1) what the committee tried to do, and could not do, and why it failed; (2) what the committee succeeded in doing; (3) what the committee wants to do; (4) what help the committee would like from the other members in carrying on its work.

Discuss each report before going on to the next. The president should be ready to start this discussion with some suggestive thought. Indeed, it is best for the president before coming to the executive committee meeting to run over in his mind the list of committees, and fix on some one matter to bring up in connection with each. It may be a plan for the future, or a hint of improvement along some line, or a word of praise for what has been done—something to set the members of the committee to talking about that work.

A model committee will not send its chairman to the executive committee meeting without some definite, practical plans to propose for its work, or at

least some perplexity to present for their solution.
As each report is made, bear in mind what was decided at the last meeting concerning that particular
kind of work, and see that in some way the success
or the failure of last month's plans is presented to
the committee and discussed. Progress is more surely
gained by sticking to a few points than by proposing
many plans. As the new suggestions are brought
up, do not let any one of them pass without nailing
it by a motion ; put it in concrete form on the
record book. At the close of the reports, the president will do well to summarize all of these determi-
nations by way of review, fixing in the minds of the
committee a sort of programme for the next month's
work.

Now and then in the course of these reports,
when any subject of special importance comes up,
or when a report is given from any line of work in
which the members are especially interested, stay
the proceedings until an earnest prayer has been
offered for just the one committee or just the special
service.

Hear next from the officers. The treasurer will
tell how faithfully the members are paying up their
pledges. The corresponding secretary will place before the committee whatever communications have
come from the outside world, and pastor and committee will decide whether they will go any farther,
and what is to be done with them. The secretary
will state the result of the last consecration meeting
roll-call. The Junior superintendent will tell about
her beautiful work, and will lay before the commit-

tee for their advice whatever important plans she has for the future. The president will say a few words on the general tone of the society and any plans he may have that have not come under the committee reports. Finally, the pastor will speak for a few minutes on the ways in which the young people may be brought closer to Christ and be more faithful in His service. The pastor, of course, has been taking part with the others throughout the evening, but this is his special opportunity for words of helpfulness, of wise suggestion, strong inspiration, and cheering praise.

Bring the meeting to a prompt close. Do not allow it to "fray out at the edge." When the reports have all been made, and if no one has general business to introduce additional to what would naturally come under the reports from chairmen and officers, ask the pastor to offer prayer, and with that prayer close the formal session of the committee.

I strongly recommend, however, that the members be not permitted to return to their homes at this point, but that you draw them still closer together with some game or other social entertainment. Pass around a plate of apples. Adjourn to the kitchen and pull molasses candy. A half-hour of fun together will not be out of place, but it will give your committee a mutual acquaintance that will do wonders for their spiritual work.

Then, when the first move is made to go, draw the happy band of Endeavorers together around the piano, sing some of the good old hymns of the church, repeat the Mizpah benediction, and separate with the love of Christ and zeal for His blessed service burning brightly in your hearts.

It only remains to add that the report of the executive committee meetings, if made to the society at all, should be made by the secretary, and should be very brief, taking up only those points that are not covered by the reports of the other committees.

CHAPTER XIV.

THE BUSINESS MEETING.

IT is far better that the monthly business meeting should not be held on Sunday in connection with the prayer meeting. This is not because there is anything in it that is not appropriate to the Lord's Day, but because all the time is needed for the prayer meeting, and a good business meeting should occupy a full hour by itself. It is coming to be a widespread custom, therefore, to hold the business meeting in connection with the monthly social, and this plan has very much to commend it. One hour for the business meeting, followed by one hour for the social—this can easily be compassed ; your social is given solid worth and dignity, and you have secured your attendance on the business meeting.

Another capital way of gaining the same end is to hold the business meeting at some private house. All will come, for the novelty of it, and out of compliment to the host or hostess. After the opening exercises, the committees will separate and discuss their various interests, including the reports soon to be presented. The society will next come together and listen to those reports, discussing each as it is given. Some pleasant general exercises will close the evening.

Refreshments? Yes, perhaps; but let them come as a surprise.

If the business meeting *must* be held on Sunday, make sure of written reports, and that they shall be brief. If any chairman fails to bring a written report, make it a rule to refuse to hear him, postponing his report to the next week's meeting, when he must bring it, written. The reason for this requirement is that the reports will be better if written, and they can then be preserved by the secretary. Besides, a written report is a formal affair, and it is not so easy to say in black and white, "Our committee has done nothing this month," as it is to rattle it off by word of mouth.

What is a good committee report? It will tell four things: what the committee planned to do; what it succeeded in doing; what it wants to do during the next month; and how the society can help it. A good report will have much earnest thought in it, and it will not be without a spice of fun. It will be written in the best English the writer can command, and with such care as befits this very important Christian service.

Provide time for the discussion of each report, the president leading, or getting some member to lead. This is the opportunity of the members to present what thoughts they may have on the work of the society, or to describe work they would like to see undertaken. If there is not time thus to discuss all the lines of committee work, only a part may be taken up at each meeting. Indeed, occasionally it may be best to focus the interest of the business meeting upon a single committee. After the reports have all been read, a paper may be presented treating the work of that committee, and this may be followed by an open parliament on the same. Whenever the society is about to launch out on some important enterprise, as, for instance, the purchase of a society library, or the adoption of the envelope pledge system of giving to missions, devote in this way one business meeting to the new departure.

Intersperse among the reports a few songs, choosing in each case a hymn appropriate to the work of the committee that has just spoken. Also now and then have a prayer, or a series of sentence prayers, whenever a committee report is especially earnest or treats of particularly important work.

The great secret of a successful business meeting is to obtain for it some fresh interest, some rememberable and advertisable (to coin a word) point. And then advertise it. Name the meeting: "A Forward-March Meeting" (to advocate the starting of a mission Sunday school, perhaps); "A 'Feed-My-Lambs' Meeting" (to discuss the condition of the Junior society); "A Next-Step Meeting" (in the interest of the lookout committee, who are anxious to bring the associates into active membership, and to get some of the active members to do better prayer-meeting work); "A Good-Samaritan Meeting" (which will propose some novel work in the hospitals). Get out attractive "dodgers" to call attention to this business meeting. And, by-the-way, does your society own a hectograph, or, still better, could it not well afford a printing press? Just

think how much it might do for the church if it had
a little printing press at its command !

One striking feature is enough to call attention to
the business meeting. It might be a union business
meeting with the Juniors. It might be the reading
of a society paper, which, with the interjection of a
little fun, will chiefly treat in a serious way the
work of the society. It might be some special
music. It might be a question-box on society prob-
lems or general religious matters. It might be an
answer-box, some important query being pro-
pounded, and each Endeavorer writing a reply.
These replies will be anonymous, and will all be read
by one person, or by a few. A good question would
be : "What are some ways in which our society
work might be bettered ? " On another occasion
some bright speaker may be obtained from outside
the town, and may close the meeting with a twenty-
minute talk. Or some good writer among the Endeavorers may read a practical essay on some such
topic as "Our Reasonable Excuses." Or there may
be an open parliament, led by your brightest member,
on some such theme as: "How can we have better
meetings?" "How get the most out of our daily
Bible-reading ? " "What suggestions have you for
some committee not your own?" "What are the
gains from the pledge?"

It is a very good plan to open the business meeting
in such a way as to show at once that no ordinary
meeting is to be held. Arrange the chairs in a
circle, with the president in the center. Or, open
with a song by some committee, the words having

reference to that committee's work. Or, open with a recitation, with an application to Christian Endeavor work.

A proper order—if you want a regular order—would be: Opening prayer. Reading of the last minutes, and approval. Unfinished business, if any. Committee reports, with discussion, if any. New business. Special order. Closing prayer and adjournment. The president will keep the meeting sharply to time, and there is no better way of doing this than by arranging beforehand for some Endeavorer to bring up each important point and be ready to present the subject and make a motion. Do not, however, allow the meeting to be too cut-and-dried to provide space for business unplanned for, since sometimes the most valuable suggestions come in this way.

Do not be satisfied if only a few make the motions. Hold before the business meeting the same ideal that we hold before our prayer meetings,—namely, that all shall take part. If the members seem dull and do not even vote, or vote in a lackadaisical way, stop the meeting short and get them on their feet to sing, or have them read a hymn in concert, or (if it is not Sunday) make them applaud some sentiment —anything to wake them up.

If, on the other hand, they are a little too wide-awake, if some proposition has aroused strong opposition, and a bit of temper has been exhibited, never forget what "the table" is for, and lay away the subject upon that secure receptacle until the society comes nearer unanimity. Heated debate should never be permitted in a Christian Endeavor society.

At the close of the meeting, a word from the president summing up the most important pieces of business that have been transacted, just to refresh the minds of the members, is very helpful, and then the meeting should close in some beautiful and inspiring way—with a prayer service, or a song service, or an earnest word from the pastor. Send the members away with the consciousness that it is the King's business they have been discussing, and that their lives should put on something of the majesty of their exalted tasks.

CHAPTER XV.

A SUMMARY OF PARLIAMENTARY LAW FOR ENDEAVORERS.

OUR Christian Endeavor business meetings and the sessions of the executive committee afford absolutely no occasion for intricate parliamentary practice. The simplest modes of procedure, the most ordinary rules of order, will suffice for the conduct of our Christian Endeavor affairs. There are no warring parties or factions in our assemblies for us to hold in check. Our business is right to the point, easily expressed, readily understood, promptly disposed of. I have never heard even of a Christian Endeavor society going into committee of the whole. We do not move "the previous question." It is about as complicated a proceeding as we indulge in, if we lay a motion on the table.

Nevertheless, the forms we do use we want to use correctly, and our societies, though they do not and should not go far in the science of parliamentary law, should go properly as far as they go. The King's business must be conducted on the very best models. For the guidance, then, of all Christian Endeavor officers who may not have access to a full parliamentary manual, such as Robert's or Cushing's, or who may not wish to spend the time necessary to pick from their many pages the few directions they need, it seems best to include in this handbook a brief summary of all the rules of order likely to be needed in presiding over Christian Endeavor business meetings.

"**The Chair.**"—The president should always refer to himself as "the chair." He should not use the first person.

"**The Floor.**"—To obtain the floor, that is, to get the right of addressing the society, a member should always rise and say, "Mr. President" (or "Miss President" or "Madam President," according as an unmarried or married lady is in the chair). He should not speak until he is recognized, the president announcing his name. If more than one claims the floor at the same time, the president should recognize the one first to speak, unless he has already spoken on the question and the other person has not.

"**Seconding Motions.**"—The president may require every motion to be seconded; but if the matter is one of little importance, he may assume a second, to save time. If any one objects, however, he must require a second. The seconder, strictly speaking, should arise and address the chair, waiting to be recognized. Practically, however, neither is required, but "I second the motion," from the seat is sufficient.

Changing a Motion.—After a motion has been seconded and stated, the consent of the seconder is required, and afterwards the consent of the society, before the mover can change it in any way.

Motions in Writing.—When a motion is long and

hard to carry in mind, the president always has the right to require the mover to submit it in writing. This, however, is a clog on the meeting, and should be done only when necessary.

Stating the Question.—Before he permits any debate, the president should state the question, saying, "It is moved and seconded that——," and following this statement with the call, "Are there any remarks?"

Rise.—Good form requires the presiding officer to rise when stating a question or putting it to vote, unless the membership is very small.

Putting the Question.—There are several common modes of putting a question to vote. The president may say, "You have heard the question. All in favor will please say, 'Aye'; all opposed, 'No.'" Or, "It has been moved and seconded that. . . . As many as are in favor of the motion will manifest it by raising the hand. Opposed, by the same sign." After the result has been announced: "The motion is carried," or, "The noes have it." Any member may rise and demand a "division." In that case the voters must rise and be counted, and the president may appoint two tellers to count for him. The chairman may vote, in case of a tie. If his vote would make a tie, he may vote, and so defeat the motion.

How Long Debatable.—A question is open to debate even after the affirmative is put, but not after the negative is put.

Casting the Vote of the Society.—When a constitution requires a vote by ballot, and for any reason the society does not wish to take the time for this, some member may move that the secretary cast the vote of the society. If the vote is carried, the secretary writes his vote upon a piece of paper, and announces it.

"If There Is No Objection."—The president may often permit procedures that are not strictly parliamentary, after giving the society an opportunity to object. For instance, after a motion has once been stated by the chair, it is unparliamentary to change its wording ; but if the society does not object, the motion may be changed by the consent of the maker and seconder, and thus much time may be saved. In the same way, the president may settle many points without the formality of a motion, saying, for instance, " Owing to the lateness of the hour, if there is no objection, we will defer to next week's meeting the reading of the remaining reports." The president will take care not to do this so often as to seem to be " bossing " the society, and he may well confine such suggestions to points upon which the society is evidently unanimous, and to occasions when the meeting is pressed for time.

The President's Informal Suggestions.—It is allowable also for the president of a Christian Endeavor society to propose items of business, or suggest courses of action, while in the chair, though in bodies more strictly parliamentary he would need to call his vice-president to the chair and speak from the floor in order to do this. For instance, if some one proposes that the society invite the local union to hold its next meeting with them, the president might say that the consent of the church officers is necessary, and add, " Will not some one make a motion appointing a committee to obtain this consent to invite the local union, and to arrange all the details for the evening of the union meeting ? "

Presidental Modesty.—Whenever a motion is made that has reference to the president in any way, the maker of the motion should put it to vote ; and if he does not do so, the president may ask him to.

Points of Order.—If any member observes, or thinks he observes, any infraction of a rule, he may rise and say, without waiting to be recognized, "Mr. President, I rise to a point of order "; upon which he immediately takes his seat. The president says, "State your point of order "; whereupon he rises, states it, and resumes his seat. The president decides the point, and his decision stands unless an appeal is taken. If the president does not choose to decide the point, he may at once call for a vote, putting the question, " Is the member in order ? Those that so judge will say, ' Aye.' Contrary minded, ' No.' "

An Appeal.—If any member objects to a ruling of the president, he rises and says, "I appeal from the decision of the chair." If this appeal is seconded, the president must at once put the question, " Is the decision of the chair sustained ? " A tie vote is counted favorable to the chair. Before putting the question, the president may, if he pleases, state the grounds for his decision ; but if the appeal refers to a matter of parliamentary practice, it is not debatable otherwise.

The Previous Question.—"I move the previous question," is the proper way to seek a close of debate and an immediate vote on the point at issue. So far as our simple Christian Endeavor practice is concerned, it takes precedence of every motion but to lay on the table. Generally a two-thirds vote is necessary to close the debate in this peremptory way. Practically, in our business meetings, when it is evident to a member that the society is ready for a vote, he calls out, " Question." If others repeat the call, or even if he himself thinks that the society is ready for a vote, the president puts the question at once. If, however, there is any objection, the stricter rule must be enforced. " The previous question " (a very misleading term) is put thus : " Shall the main question be now put ? "

Laying on the Table.—If a member wishes to postpone a subject so that it may be taken up at a later time, he moves that it be laid on the table, and this motion is undebatable. When it is desired to consider the matter, the motion is made " to take the question from the table." And this motion also may not be debated.

Postponement.—If it is desired to defer the matter with less freedom, a motion may be made to postpone to a certain time, in which case only a two-thirds vote can take up the question before that time ; or to postpone the subject indefinitely, which, if carried, makes it impossible to take up the matter again during the session.

Amendments.—If it is desired to change a motion

in any particular, to make additions to it or subtract from it, or even to substitute another motion on the same subject, it is done by a motion to amend, the mover saying, "Mr. President, I move to amend the motion before the society by adding ...." or " by striking out the words,.............. " or " by inserting the words, ... before ...." or " by substituting for it the following motion ...." The amendment may exactly reverse the first motion, or change it only slightly. The mover of the motion, with the consent of his second, may, if no one objects, accept the amendment without a vote. An amendment may be amended, but not the amendment of an amendment. In voting, the president will first put the amendment to the amendment; then, if that is lost, he will put the first amendment; and if it is carried, he will put the first amendment as amended. If that is lost, he will put the original motion; and if it is carried, he will put the original motion as amended by one or both of the amendments. No amendment is allowed in case of a motion to adjourn, to lay on the table, to postpone indefinitely, to reconsider, or to call for the previous question.

Reconsidering a Subject.—If any person who voted with the prevailing side desires, he may move the reconsideration of a subject upon which the society has voted, provided the motion to reconsider is made at the meeting when the vote was taken. The motion cannot be amended, and may be debated only when the motion to be reconsidered was debatable. If carried, it puts the subject back where it was before the vote upon it was taken.   A motion to reconsider, therefore, if carried, makes possible more debate on the original motion, and requires a new vote upon it. No question can be reconsidered more than once.

A Motion to Adjourn.—A motion to adjourn must be put at once, no matter what subject is under discussion; and it cannot be debated, nor can the vote be reconsidered.

Committees.—A very common and useful way of disposing of a matter upon which further light should be thrown before the society can judge wisely concerning it, is to vote "that the subject be referred to a committee." The mover of the motion may state of how many the committee is to consist, and how they are to be appointed, whether by the nomination and election of the society, or, as is more customary, by the chair.   If the president is to appoint, he may at once state who are to form the committee, or he may take. time to consider, if it is an important committee, and give its membership later in the meeting, or even at another meeting, unless the society direct otherwise. The first person named upon a committee is its chairman, and must call the committee together and see that it is organized.   Usually he is made the permanent chairman. Often the mover of the motion to commit the subject is made chairman of the committee, but this is a dangerous custom to establish, since the maker of the motion is not always the best available chairman, and besides, many are prevented from making necessary motions by fear of seeming to seek this honor.   If the maker of the motion to commit did not include in his motion a statement of the number of which the committee shall consist, and of how it is to be appointed, then, after the subject has been committed, the president asks, "Of how many shall this committee consist?" And after the maker of the motion or the society has answered, he will then ask, "How shall this committee be appointed?" These matters are usually decided informally and without a vote.

The Call of a Committee Meeting.—If the chairman of a committee is absent, or will not call a meeting, any two members of the committee may call it together.

Committee Reports. — When a committee is ready to report, the chairman so states, and a motion that the report be received may be made, or the president may call for it without such a motion. The formal methods of beginning the reports, such as, "The committee on —— beg leave to submit the following report," and the formal mode of closing a report, "All of which is respectfully submitted," may often be profitably varied, in our Christian Endeavor reports, in the interest of sprightliness. After the report is read, the committee is discharged thereby, unless it is presented as a partial report. It is not customary to vote upon accepting (or "adopting"— the two terms have the same force) the report of a standing Christian Endeavor committee, though the report of any committee, standing or special, should be adopted or rejected if it contains a recommendation for the society's action. The better way, in the case of a standing committee, usually is to receive the report and place it on file, and then by a separate motion to vote upon the recommendation it contains. If the society pleases, it may refuse to act upon the recommendation, and " recommit " the subject, in which case the committee just discharged by the reception of its report is restored to life again.

Standing and Special Committees.—A standing committee is one appointed for some definite time; a " special committee " is one appointed for a particular purpose. It would add to the interest of our Christian Endeavor business if more occasions were found for the appointment of special committees.

CHAPTER XVI.

RECEPTION AND INSTALLATION SERVICES.

THERE is little danger that our Christian Endeavor officers will become overzealous and conceited; there is enough to keep them humble. There is far more danger that they may not "magnify their office" and understand their responsibility. The best way of impressing upon them the greatness and blessedness of the task they have undertaken is by a public installation service. This service is best conducted in the society meeting room, and as part of the regular prayer meeting, though announcement of it should be made beforehand, and the older church members should be invited to attend. The pastor himself, as will be seen, figures largely in the service I suggest, but if the church is temporarily without a pastor, some church officer or prominent church worker will take his part.

Service for the Installation of Officers.

[The pastor and the retiring officers are seated together on the platform. The retiring president presides, and opens the meeting by calling for three hearty Christian Endeavor hymns in swift succession. One of the retiring officers, selected by the president, then reads our Christian Endeavor work-

8

ers' chapter of the Bible, the twelfth of Romans. This is followed by a brief prayer by some other officer chosen by the president, or by the president himself. The retiring president, addressing the pastor, then speaks to the following effect, though he may prefer to use his own words.]

The President.—At the close of the term of office to which we were elected by our Christian Endeavor society, we, the officers, now lay down our commissions. Doubtless we have made many mistakes. Doubtless we have fallen far short of our possible successes. We pray God to forgive us for all sins of omission and commission. We lay at His feet our imperfect service, asking Him to work out from it His own perfect results.

The Pastor (varying the words, as all the words of this exercise may be varied, to suit his pleasure or changed circumstances).—Will the officers and committee chairmen please rise? (They rise, remaining standing, each where he is.) I praise God, dear friends, and this Christian Endeavor society praises God, for all your faithful service. Whatever you have done for Christ has brought with it, we are certain, its abundant and immediate reward. By every act of firm fidelity to duty, by every unselfish yielding of your will, by every effort you have made during your term of office to increase the efficiency of this society and draw its members nearer to their Saviour, you have yourselves become strengthened and ennobled. As you now lay down your official responsibilities, we give you our hearty God-speed upon the path of endeavor that still lies before you, and in token of our appreciation of your work I now call upon the entire society to rise and sing one stanza of our Christian Endeavor harvest hymn, " Bringing in the Sheaves."

[This is done, and then the retiring officers leave the platform, all but the president.]

Pastor.—Mr. President, you will please present the officers-elect.

[The president reads the list, stating with each name the office to be filled. As the several persons are named, they come forward and stand in a semicircle in front of the pulpit. The retiring president then takes his seat in the audience.]

Pastor.—Endeavorers, the tasks you are now by vote of this society to assume are tasks which, though simple in their elements, reach out into all eternity. They have to do with the making of character, and there is no more blessed or momentous task than the making of character. You have been given a great privilege, you have entered a glorious opportunity. As you lead these members faithfully along the highways of Christian Endeavor, both you and they will be strengthened. I exhort you not to trust in your own wisdom, but to seek divine guidance, for that alone will render you workmen that need not to be ashamed. I exhort you not to rest satisfied with the present attainments of the society, but to make " Excelsior " your motto. This society has chosen you to serve them in their highest interests, and I urge you to undertake the task in the spirit of Him whose you are and whom you serve. In token that you will do this, will you not repeat after me His own words : "The Son of Man came not to be ministered unto, but to minister."

[The officers repeat this in concert.]

The Pastor.—And now, Mr. President, you will please present the newly elected chairmen of committees.

[The new president reads the list, and each chairman, as his name is called, rises and remains standing.]

The Pastor.—There is no branch of our society work, Endeavorers, that will not during the coming months receive the impulse of your zeal, if you are faithful, or the hindrance of your sloth, if you are faithless. It is our glad expectation that under your wise and vigorous guidance our society is to take many advance steps this term. Seek out the best methods. Read the most practical books. Consult the most skilful workers. Take your tasks constantly to God in prayer. Do not leave the little things neglected in your pursuit of some large achievement, yet do not so bury yourself in details that you forget the wider interests. Remember Paul, and like him resolve to be all things to all men, that by all means you may save some one soul. And in token of your determination in Christ's strength to do your best, I call upon you to repeat with me one of Paul's great sayings : "I can do all things through Christ who strengtheneth me."

[The chairmen repeat this in concert. The pastor then takes his seat in the audience, together with all the others except the new president.]

The President.—And now, as an indication of our

desire as a united society to reach these high ideals of service and reward, let us all rise and sing together one stanza of "To the Work."

[This is done, and then the president speaks again.]

The President.—Now, at the outset of this new term's work, it is most appropriate to emphasize our allegiance to the fundamental principles of this society. Let us all remain standing and repeat in concert the Christian Endeavor pledge.

[After this the president again speaks.]

The President.—Let us all bow our heads and in silence for a few moments ask our unseen Leader for His blessing upon the work we are about to undertake together. Following the silent prayer I will lead in a series of sentence prayers, in which many will voice our petitions for all our society activities; and then our pastor will close this service with a prayer of consecration.

[The regular prayer meeting follows, the leader for the evening taking his place at the desk.]

Reception Services.

The practical experience of a multitude of societies has proved the value of a little ceremony in receiving new members. Membership in the society means much more to members thus received, and they are more faithful to the pledge. There is only one danger—that the service may seem to imitate the service used in joining the church. For that reason I would carefully avoid all phrases customarily found in church reception services, the use of

the song, "Blest be the tie that binds," "the right
hand of fellowship," and, in fact, everything that
might be considered even an indirect allusion to
that most solemn service. Care is taken in the following suggested forms to avoid this possible objection, and these exercises, while earnest and impressive, will not be thought by any one to be trenching
on the field of the church, or rendering common-
place one of its most sacred ceremonies.

This reception of new members should come at
regular intervals, and it is better that it should
always fall on consecration meetings. The president
will be in the chair, and he will ask the secretary to
call the names of the new members. If they were
elected at the last meeting, they will come forward
as their names are called; but if their names were
proposed at the last meeting, the president will put
their election to vote, and after election they will
come forward. Then will follow this little ceremony.

The Reception of Active Members.

The President (addressing the new members, as
they stand before him).—You have signified your desire to join this society. Having read our constitution and the Christian Endeavor pledge, you have
said to the lookout committee that you wish to work
in accordance with the constitution, and that you
will keep the requirements of the pledge. With this
understanding, the society has gladly by its vote accepted you among its members. In ratification of
all this, let all the Endeavorers rise and repeat with

these new members our Christian Endeavor covenant.

[The society rises, and joins the new members in
repeating the pledge, the president leading.]

The President.—While we remain standing, let us
testify our joy at receiving these new members, and
our sense of our fellowship in Christian Endeavor,
by singing one stanza of a welcome song, "Stand
up, stand up for Jesus." While we are singing, the
secretary will present the constitution, and each
candidate will sign it in the presence of the society.

[Choose some other welcome song, if your hymn-
book contains a preferable one. The secretary
should be ready with the constitution and pen and
ink, at a table in front of the society. This public
signing of the constitution, including, of course, the
pledge, always serves to impress upon the new
members the vows they are taking. Sing as many
stanzas as are necessary to occupy the time of signing.]

The President.—It is the custom of our society to
give to each new member a Christian Endeavor pin,
in the hope that it will serve as an earnest of our
brotherly affection, and as a constant reminder of
the covenant you have just repeated with us. We
ask that you show your Christian Endeavor colors
faithfully, and we pray that this little emblem may
come to mean as much in your lives as it means in
ours.

[Of course, if this gift of a pin is not customary in
your society, the foregoing will be omitted. It is a
delightful and most helpful practice, however, and I
earnestly recommend it.]

The President, after presenting the pins, goes on to say : It is also the custom of this society to present to each new member a copy of this book, " The Christian Endeavor Greeting." In it you will find a statement of the purposes of our society and a summary of its methods. It will tell you how to be helpful to us, and how to gain help from the society. We ask you to read it carefully, and to adopt it as your Christian Endeavor guide-book.

[This " Christian Endeavor Greeting " is published in most attractive form by the United Society of Christian Endeavor. It is in large, handsome type, and may be obtained, bound prettily in paper, for ten cents, or a dollar a dozen, There is also a special gift edition, bound daintily, in white cloth, with a handsome stamp and with gilt top ; this costs twenty-five cents, or five for one dollar. This presentation edition is the one the society should use if it can afford it, and twenty or twenty-five cents is very little to spend upon each new member. Send for a sample of the book, and you will see how practically useful it is. Of course, the foregoing is to be omitted if the society does not put the "Greeting" into the hands of its new members.]

The President.—You are now Christian Endeavorers, and we welcome you into our goodly fellowship. It is a fellowship as wide as the earth. It includes young people of all races and climes and nations, from the Zulus to the Esquimaux, from China to Brazil, from England, France, and Germany to Hawaii, New Zealand, and Japan.

This precious fellowship includes also the young

people of all evangelical denominations. "We are not divided, all one body we." The Christian Endeavor unions, of which you have become a part, will cause you to realize as you may never have realized before the grandeur of Christ's great church universal.

It is a fellowship of service that you have entered, a fellowship in Christian endeavor. We trust that you will do your part, and more than your part, in all our society work. To emphasize this principle of service, it is our custom to assign to each new member, as soon as he joins, a place on some committee, and your committee assignments are as follows : . . . .

[Of course if your society does not place every member upon some committee, the foregoing sentences will be omitted ; but if you try the plan, you will not give it up.]

Finally, Endeavorers, we welcome you into a fellowship of faith. The first sentence of our pledge is the great one. It is because we trust in the Lord Jesus for strength, that we are trying to do whatever He would like to have us do. Only as we have fellowship with Him in our daily prayer and Bible-reading, can our fellowship with one another be a fellowship of Christian endeavor. It is our prayer that you may come to know every day more and more fully the power of the presence of Christ. Please be seated, and listen to a word from our pastor.

[The new members will sit in the front row of seats, and the pastor will welcome them and give them some kindly advice in regard to their religious life and their Christian Endeavor duties. If your church has no pastor, substitute for this service the best person available.]

The President.—Now, fellow Endeavorers, in receiving these new members, have we no duty to perform, do we assume no responsibility? In a moment of silent prayer, let us ask God to bless their relation to us and ours to them, and then let a number follow me in sentence prayers for God's blessing upon this society and these new members in all their Christian endeavors. I will ask our pastor to close the sentence prayers with a prayer of consecration.

The Reception of Associate Members.

[This should be much briefer and simpler. There may be the gift of the pin and of the "Greeting," and the appointment to some of the minor committees, but there is no pastor's greeting unless active members are received at the same time. After the associate members have been voted in, the president will call them forward, and will say :—]

The President.—We rejoice that God has put it in your hearts to desire fellowship with this society of Christian Endeavor. The associates' pledge, which you are ready to sign, obligates you to attend our meetings faithfully, and we trust that we may be helpful to you in every way; but especially that through our meetings you may come to know our Saviour, and to join His church, becoming His professed followers. To that end, the society will both work and pray. May God bless you as you sign our associate roll during the singing of the hymn.

The Reception of Honorary Members.

The honorary members *ex officiis*, the pastor and church officers, will not be given formal reception, since they are all members of the society by virtue of their office, but it would be pleasant to signalize in some public way the addition of other members to the honorary l: st. They take no pledge, and the gift of the pin and "Greeting" would not be very appropriate, so that the form just given would not be suitable. I advise, however, that no form be used; that the honorary members be not called before the society at all, but merely that, they being present, their accession shall be announced, while the pastor gives them, on behalf of the young people, a word of greeting, and tells them what are their privileges and duties in connection with the society.

The Reception of Juniors.

When you are receiving graduates from the Junior society into active or associate membership, you *may* use the forms just given without change, but it is far better to make some special recognition of the Juniors, for the sake of those left in the Junior society whom you wish to teach to look forward to entrance into the ranks of the older Endeavorers. Invite the entire Junior society to be present. Once a year the uniform topics give us a union meeting of the two societies, and this is the best time for the transfer of members. The portions of the reception service that are different from that just given are the following.

The president of the Young People's society sits on the platform with the president of the Junior society.

The President.—(to the Junior president).—I am glad to welcome you as the representative of our comrade branch of Christian Endeavor, our younger brother, the Junior society, and I am especially glad as you bring to us the gift of new members. Please present them to the society.

[Here the Junior president reads the list of candidates, who step forward as their names are called. If they have not already been voted in, the president puts the matter to vote at this juncture. If other members are to be received at this time, call them forward, and proceed without further reference to the Juniors, but if the Juniors alone are to be received, the president of the Young People's society may go on as follows.]

The President.—We count ourselves especially fortunate in adding to our number those that have already received training in Christian Endeavor methods and principles. You have learned in the Junior society the value of a pledge, and you have proved yourselves able to keep a covenant. You have had a drill in committee work. You have found out the joy of public testimony for Christ. Doubtless you are sorry to part from the many pleasant associations of the Junior society, but we trust that all such losses will be more than made good by your joy in enlarged activities and higher and harder service. To this we welcome you. Christian Endeavor's word is, "Forward!" Having taken this step, we trust that you will go on to take many more steps in advance, till you reach the blessed goal of all Christian Endeavor. You have advanced from a simple pledge to one that is more inclusive, and I ask you, in token that your spirits are joined with ours in seeking the great aims of our covenant, to unite your vows with ours as all rise and repeat together the Christian Endeavor pledge.

[From this point the service is the same as that already given, except that "Onward, Christian Soldiers" would perhaps be a better song to sing while the Juniors are signing the membership roll.]

CHAPTER XVII.

THE USE OF LITERATURE.

THE success of a Christian Endeavor society depends so largely upon its wise use of Christian Endeavor literature, and the use of this literature depends so much on the officers' activity in this direction, that a chapter on the subject is necessary in an officers' handbook. Too many societies, instead of standing as they might stand on the shoulders of all the other societies that have done good work, profiting by their experience, adopting the best of their methods, and incorporating the enthusiasm of their successes, choose weakly to live to themselves, cackling over their petty discoveries that became ancient news in wide-awake societies ten years ago, and plodding along with antique methods that have been superseded by far better ways of working.

One of the chief advantages of our interdenominational Christian Endeavor fellowship is that it provides a means for gathering up in one center of information the best that is planned and achieved in young people's religious work all over the world. This center is the United Society of Christian Endeavor, and the society that makes no use, or slight use, of its literature, receives only a small part of the gains to be derived from membership in our movement. This literature has now become remarkably complete, inspiring, and practically useful. It includes books and pamphlets on all kinds of committee work, and all the various lines of activity taken up in our societies and their unions. It includes whole libraries, or single volumes. It includes large books, or mere leaflets. It includes treatises for the advanced worker, and primers for the beginner. It includes an international organ for the older societies, *The Christian Endeavor World*, and one for the Junior societies, *The Junior Christian Endeavor World*. It includes song-books and exercises, and charts and cards of all kinds, and blank books and topic cards, and devotional helps and missionary libraries, and stories and poems, and Christian Endeavor histories and Christian Endeavor travels, and Christian Endeavor year books. When the Christian Endeavor movement began, in 1881, there was no literature dealing with religious work among the young. Now, thanks to the labors of the United Society of Christian Endeavor—labors, as all should know, that are entirely self-supporting—this literature is one of the most complete in the world. Whatever the need, the publication department of the United Society is prepared at the invitation of a postal-card to supply it promptly.

It would be a pleasure to give here a list, for each committee, of the books, pamphlets, exercises, and other helps especially prepared for its particular line of work, but such a list would be inadequate almost before this book was off the press, so rapidly are improvements made, and so many are the additions to the growing catalogue. The only practical thing to do is to urge every reader of this book to ask the United Society (Tremont Temple, Boston) to send the most recent price-list, which, of course, will be sent free. You will be astonished at the number, variety, and cheapness of the helps there enumerated.

It would also be a pleasure, of course, to give here an account of *The Christian Endeavor World*, but this, too, is improving all the time, and the helpful and attractive features I might name to-day will be " back numbers " to-morrow as truly as this week's issue will be a " back number " next week. The only way to get an idea of what our international Christian Endeavor organ is, is to send a postal-card request for free sample copies,—its address also being Tremont Temple, Boston.

" Oh, it will cost too much," I hear some societies say. In the first place, investigate, and you will find that these books and pamphlets are sold at a cost remarkably low. Only the slightest profit is made upon each copy. And even when compared with the published novels that are sold by the hundred thousand copies, these Christian Endeavor publications will be seen to be wonderfully inexpensive.

One of the best ways to get the literature of the United Society is by ordering a complete supply of whatever your committees need in the way of committee helps. The United Society is able to sell these sets of books and pamphlets at much less even than the ordinary low prices for single copies. An entertainment may be got up for the purpose of raising the necessary money, or it may be obtained by private subscription (do not forget the honorary members !), or each committee may be asked to buy its own helps for its own use and for handing down to succeeding committees, or the society may appropriate from its treasury the necessary sum. You should have a good-literature committee, and it should be one of their main objects to get our Christian Endeavor literature into the hands of all the Endeavorers.

Then, how to get it read and used ! For not merely the officers should read it, but all the chairmen ; and not only the chairmen, but their committee members and all the society. The literature itself will answer this question. One of the best plans is to hold, after the books and pamphlets have arrived, a literature night, taking the place possibly of some social. On this occasion every member will speak briefly on some good plan he has seen described in some of the new books and pamphlets, and there will be a discussion upon each to see whether it is adapted to your society. One of the best ways to use *The Christian Endeavor World*—especially the copy or copies taken by the society for its prayer-meeting leaders and other workers—is to appoint a scrapbook committee, which will take the papers after the prayer-meeting leader is through with them, and cut them up, sorting out the articles into piles for the various committees according to their themes. These clippings will be given to the committees and pasted in committee scrapbooks, or

9

filed in envelopes for immediate use or future reference.

No society ever made such use of Christian Endeavor literature as I have here advised, without finding its work greatly stimulated in all departments, its meetings more lively and attractive and spiritual, its gifts increased, and more souls won for the Master.

CHAPTER XVIII.

THE SOCIETY AND THE CHURCH.

IT is absurd to think that there should be any jealousy of the Christian Endeavor society on the part of the church, or any suspicion of the church on the part of the society. The society *is* the church—it is the church in one of its most important functions, the church training its young. Discord between the two is as if the eye and the hand should quarrel, and it is not to be thought of for a moment. Where there is any trouble of the kind, it is because the fundamental ideas of the Christian Endeavor Society have been lost from sight, and it is the duty of the church, as the older body of Christians, to hold its young people true to those ideals.

I am writing now, however, for Christian Endeavor officers, and the question is, What should you be doing to keep the society close to the church and loyal to its interests, and at the same time preserve and increase the interest of the older Christians in the society?

The pastor is, of course, the chief factor in the situation. Invite him to become an active member. If he thinks best not to do this, give him all the rights of an honorary member. Note also how many times and on what various occasions he is to be consulted, in accordance with the constitution. Make him know that he is really wanted at the executive committee meetings. Assure him that he will be an honored and welcome visitor at any meeting of any committee. Go to him and ask him to give the society some work to do to help him and the church. Often invite the pastor to lead the Christian Endeavor prayer meeting. Especially, adopt the delightful and profitable custom of reserving for the pastor the last five minutes of each prayer meeting in which to sum up the teachings of the evening. He may not be able to be present at every meeting, but let him understand that this time is his whenever he is present, and then strictly instruct your leaders to call upon him five minutes before the close of the hour.

Then, there are the church services. The fact that each Endeavorer has taken a vow to be present at these, unless he has a reason Christ would accept, makes it no more a duty for the Endeavorers to attend these meetings than for their elders, since there is nothing in our pledge which is not implied or expressed in the church covenant, and I believe that the Endeavorers are actually far more faithful in these directions than the average church-member. But they are younger, and it may be held that they should be more regular attendants. At any rate, Christian Endeavor has no business to compare itself with anything but the absolute standard of perfection, nor to rest satisfied until every member attends the Sunday evening service and the midweek prayer meeting as a matter of course.

Advertise these meetings. Let the society officers often remind the members of their vows in this direction. Keep careful records of attendance, and make comparative reports from time to time. Divide the society into groups, and appoint now one group and now another to speak briefly and modestly in the church prayer meeting. Offer the services of the Endeavorers as ushers at the Sunday evening service. Ask the pastor if he would not like a Christian Endeavor choir for Sunday evening and for the church prayer meeting. If the holding of the Christian Endeavor meeting just before the Sunday evening service, as so many societies do, seems to any to draw the young people away from the latter meeting (I do not think it ever really does) make a test of the matter by boldly transferring the Endeavor meeting to a week night—which, in my judgment, is a far better time for it, any way. Take a holy pride in proving yourself true to your promise to "support your own church in every way."

The honorary membership affords a fine opportunity for cementing the relation between the society and the church, and it should be used more often and more fully than it is. Extend the list beyond the persons who are honorary members *ex-officiis*. Do not appoint men and women to honorary membership in order to interest them in the society, but interest them first and then appoint them. Cultivate the attendance of the older people at the meeting, especially of those wise Christians who know how to be brief, and even to keep silent. Go to

them, when they come, and tell them you are glad
to see them. At least once a year hold an honorary
members' meeting, led by an honorary member,
with all the honorary members present and taking
part. Be sure to give the honorary members special
invitations to the socials. Once a year hold a social
especially for the old folks of the church. Go to
your honorary members for advice, for money, for
little speeches now and then, and in every way
strive to make them feel that they are identified
with the society's activities.

The church's authority is absolute, and I think I
have never heard of a Christian Endeavor society
questioning it. Indeed, my chief quarrel with the
situation is that the church too seldom exercises
any authority, or seems to feel any responsibility
for the Christian Endeavor society. Church members occasionally indulge in criticism of the society
—though usually the criticism is kindly; but it is
not often that the church as an organism sets itself
to give aid, oversight, and inspiration to this organized body of its young people. I believe that the
Endeavor society should be represented in some
way upon the official boards of the church, and that
it should report regularly at the church meetings.
I believe that as thorough watch should be kept
over its interests as over those of the Sunday school,
and that if the Endeavor society grows weak and
inefficient, the church should know it as soon, and
take measures to restore it as vigorously as it
would if the Sunday morning congregation should
fall off. Certainly it should not be so one-sided as

that the Endeavorers should be expected to give absolute loyalty to the church while the church gives less than absolute loyalty to the best interests of the Endeavorers.

One of the finest things a society can do is to establish and carry on indefinitely some regular course of study in denominational history, missions, or doctrines. The pastor, or some experienced member of the church, should lead this class, and it might be held in connection with the society meeting, or on some other evening, according to circumstances. At any rate, such studies will do more than anything else to bind the society firmly to the church.

Thus it must be the firm purpose of every Christian Endeavor officer to permit no shadow of antagonism to arise between the society and the church. If any misapprehension comes up, see at once that it is removed. In all the ways I have suggested, and as many more as you can invent, draw the older Christians into sympathy with your work, and as far as possible into active co-operation.

A word is needed here for the benefit of the numerous societies that are not connected with any church, the "union societies" found in sparsely settled districts, meeting in country schoolhouses, and chiefly on the frontier. There is no church at hand, or if there are several churches, the membership is too small to warrant any but a union Christian Endeavor society. How much of this talk about loyalty to their church applies to such societies?

With a few obvious changes, every word I have said may be applied to those societies whose members belong to different denominations. The fact that they meet together in the Christian Endeavor prayer meeting should give them all the more zeal for their church work. If a missionary offering is received, divide it proportionately among the denominations represented, or let each Endeavorer give solely through his own church, or let the union society give to such interdenominational societies as the American Bible Society, the American Sunday-school Union, the China Inland Mission. Each Endeavorer's pledge has reference, of course, to the services in his own church, and not to the services in the church where the society happens to meet.

CHAPTER XIX.

A GLANCE AT CHRISTIAN ENDEAVOR HISTORY.

EVERY Endeavorer, but especially every Christian Endeavor officer, should know something about the history of the Christian Endeavor movement, partly because those that are ignorant regarding it will naturally come to them for information, and will gain an unfavorable opinion of the society from their failure to answer their questions, and partly because no one can understand the movement without knowing the principal events in its history, and partly because the story is an inspiring one, and a knowledge of it is an inspiration to better work. In this chapter I can give the barest outline, and for full details I must refer the reader to Dr. Clark's large volume, "World-Wide Endeavor," and to my little five-cent pamphlet, "A Short History of the Christian Endeavor Movement" (both sold by the United Society of Christian Endeavor).

The first society was established on the evening of February 2, 1881, in the Williston Church, Portland, Me., by Rev. Francis E. Clark, D.D., the original pledge and constitution being substantially the same as at present. In August of that year, the first article concerning the new society was published by *The Congregationalist*, and soon the second article was published by *The Sunday School Times*, both from Dr. Clark's pen. In October, 1881, the second society was formed by Rev. C. P. Mills, at Newbury-port, Mass.

By June 2, 1882, six societies were known, and on that date the first Christian Endeavor convention was held, in Williston Church, Portland. Other places where these early annual conventions were held are : Lowell, Mass., Old Orchard, Me., Saratoga, N. Y., Chicago, Philadelphia, St. Louis, Minneapolis. The Philadelphia Convention, in 1889, brought together 6,500 delegates, the St. Louis Convention 8,000, and the Minneapolis Convention (1891) more than 14,000, marking the beginning of the vast proportions of the movement.

During this first decade, Dr. Clark wrote the first Christian Endeavor book " Children and the Church." The movement had spread to the younger children, and the first Junior society had been formed. The United Society of Christian Endeavor had been formed (1885). The movement had reached foreign countries (China, 1885). The first local union had been organized, that of New Haven, Conn., (1886), and the first State union (also in Connecticut, 1885). The Christian Endeavor organ, *The Golden Rule*, now called *The Christian Endeavor World*, sent out its first number in October, 1886. Dr. Clark became its editor and the president of the United Society, and made in England the first of his remarkable Christian Endeavor journeys in foreign lands (1888). Christian Endeavor Day began to be celebrated (1888), General Secretary Baer was appointed to office (1889), and the revised pledge was adopted in the same year, while in 1890 Doctors Clark, Boynton, Hill, and Dickinson—foremost among Christian Endeavor pioneers—made a second Christian Endeavor tour of Great Britain. All this in the first decade.

The close of the first decade of Christian Endeavor was marked by the rise of the exclusive denominational young people's society, which threatened for a time to destroy our interdenominational fellowship, and break up the Christian Endeavor movement into scores of relatively weak and inefficient societies. Better counsels prevailed, however, and nearly all the denominational societies now receive into their full membership, without change of name or constitution, the Christian Endeavor societies of the same denomination.

The second decade of Christian Endeavor has been signalized by a growth even more wonderful than the first decade. The international conventions have surpassed all previous religious gatherings in the world's history, in their vast proportions, their unbounded enthusiasm, and their deep spiritual results. New York (1892) brought together at least 35,000 delegates ; Boston (1895) the immense number of 56,435 registered Endeavorers. The Montreal Convention of 1893 was the first held outside the United States ; the San Francisco Convention of 1897 was the first held on the Pacific coast, and fully ten thousand Endeavorers traversed the entire breadth of the country to attend it ; the Nashville Convention of 1898 was the first held in the South.

The second decade has seen a marvelous growth

of the movement in foreign lands. Much of this progress has been due to journeys undertaken by Dr. Clark, usually accompanied by Mrs. Clark, who has been especially successful in spreading the principles of the Junior society. In the course of these journeys Dr. Clark has circumnavigated the globe more than once, and has frequently visited all the leading nations of Europe, Asia, and Africa, not omitting Australia and the islands of the Pacific. Hundreds, and in some cases thousands, of societies are found in all these lands. United Societies of Christian Endeavor have been organized in Japan, China, Australia, India, South Africa, Germany, and Great Britain. These hold large and enthusiastic conventions, publish Christian Endeavor papers and other literature in all the important languages of the globe, and carry on all the Christian Endeavor activities as successfully in each case as if the society had been originally planned for that soil alone.

The first society formed outside of America was formed in the Hawaiian Islands, in 1884. China's beginning was in 1885. It was not until 1887 that the first society was formed in England, at Crewe. It was at Crewe also that the first British convention was held, in 1891. The first international convention outside the American continent was that held in London in 1900.

Of course, the growth of our Society in these various foreign lands has been attended by many interesting and remarkable events, and a fuller knowledge of these than can be given in my limited

space would inspire any Endeavorer. I might instance the secret upspringing of the Madagascar
societies, the persecutions suffered by the Armenian
societies from the Turks and by the Spanish societies from the Catholics, the missionary record of
the Samoan Endeavorers.

During this second decade, too, the society entered
the navies of the world as well as the armies, and
stirring tales are to be told of Christian Endeavor
on battleships and in camps. Especially in the war
between the United States and Spain were the
Floating societies and the societies in the army
brought into prominence. Recent years have also
seen a blessed development of Christian Endeavor
work in the State prisons and the jails. Mothers'
societies have sprung up, Senior societies among the
older Christians, and, to a notable degree, Intermediate societies, midway between the Junior and
the Young People's societies. Work among life-
savers and surfmen, among street-car men and com-
mercial travelers, has also been organized.

The societies have taken up during recent years a
number of important lines of work for the special
service of the church. Most conspicuous of these
are the movement for systematic and generous giving, known as the Tenth Legion; the movement for
the deepening of the spiritual life, known as the
Quiet Hour movement, and the Macedonian Phalanx, to stimulate interest in missions by gifts
through denominational boards to definitely known
missionaries with whom the Endeavorers are brought
into personal touch. A stronger Christian citizen-

ship, the promotion of temperance, and interna‑
tional arbitration, are also among the aims of Chris‑
tian Endeavor.   During this second decade, the
State unions organized in the first decade have gone
on to great proportions and influence. Several of
the States hold annual gatherings whose attendants
number from eight to ten thousand.

This sketch of our Christian Endeavor history, a
mere outline as it is, will serve its purpose if it sends
the reader to fuller sources of information.   Chris‑
tian Endeavor has already made a marvelous rec‑
ord.   Every year it is writing a noble chapter in its
history.   As the second decade has in every point
surpassed the first, so we may confidently expect the
third decade to surpass the second.   Whether this
shall be the case or not, will depend largely upon
the readers of this book, the officers of the local.
Christian Endeavor societies.   For all these gains
have been won for Christ and the church not by an
influential organization, not by force of authority,
not by the outpouring of money, not by the prestige
of genius.   These noble deeds have been wrought,
and thus mightily have the young people of the
world been moved for Christian Endeavor, through
the faithful activities of many thousands unknown
to fame.   Because this Christian Endeavor presi‑
dent and that Christian Endeavor secretary, this
prayer-meeting leader and that member of the look‑
out committee and yonder stammering beginner in
the Christian life have dared to take definite pledges
and have courageously lived up to them, because
they have done their best, each in his little corner,

because of that, this great thing which is not in a corner, and which nothing smaller than the world can contain, Christian Endeavor, has grown to its blessed power.   O Christian Endeavorers, it pays to be brave, though no one knows it but Christ.   It pays to try hard things, to be willing to fail, to spend time and money and thought and energy upon even the least of Christian enterprises.   For the Father, who sees in secret, will reward you openly.

www.ingramcontent.com/pod-product-compliance
Lightning Source LLC
Chambersburg PA
CBHW021155020426
42331CB00003B/74